PENGUIN BOOKS

# WILL THEY EVER TRUST US AGAIN?

Bestselling author, award-winning filmmaker, performer and activist, Michael Moore is known around the world for his work. He was born in Flint, Michigan, where he became involved in student politics and went on to make the ground-breaking documentary *Roger & Me*, which exposed how big business had destroyed his hometown. He created and hosted the Emmy-winning series *TV Nation* and *The Awful Truth*, won an Oscar for his film *Bowling for Columbine*, and his latest documentary *Fahrenheit 9/11* has won the Palme d'Or at the 2004 Cannes Film Festival, broken all box office records and been described as a 'historical landmark' (*Guardian*).

His books *Stupid White Men* and *Dude, Where's My Country?* are acclaimed international bestsellers and have sold nearly five million copies between them. Michael Moore lives with his wife and daughter in Michigan and New York. You can visit his website at www.michaelmoore.com to find out more and get involved.

D1353851

# Will They Ever Trust Us Again?

## Letters from the War Zone to Michael Moore

Michael Moore

PENGUIN BOOKS

# PENGUIN BOOKS

Published by the Penguin Group
Penguin Books Ltd, 80 Strand, London WC2R 0RL, England
Penguin Group (USA) Inc., 375 Hudson Street, New York, New York 10014, USA
Penguin Group (Canada), 90 Eglinton Avenue East, Suite 700, Toronto,
Ontario, Canada M4P 3YZ (a division of Pearson Penguin Canada Inc.)
Penguin Ireland, 25 St Stephen's Green, Dublin 2, Ireland
(a division of Penguin Books Ltd)
Penguin Group (Australia), 250 Camberwell Road, Camberwell, Victoria 3124,
Australia (a division of Pearson Australia Group Pty Ltd)
Penguin Books India Pvt Ltd, 11 Community Centre,
Panchsheel Park, New Delhi – 110 017, India
Penguin Group (NZ), cnr Airborne and Rosedale Roads, Albany,
Auckland 1310, New Zealand (a division of Pearson New Zealand Ltd)
Penguin Books (South Africa) (Pty) Ltd, 24 Sturdee Avenue,
Rosebank 2196, South Africa

Penguin Books Ltd, Registered Offices: 80 Strand, London WC2R 0RL, England

www.penguin.com

First published in the United States of America by Simon and Schuster 2004
First published in Great Britain by Allen Lane 2004
Published in Penguin Books 2005
1

Printed in England by Clays Ltd, St Ives plc

TO MY UNCLE LORNIE

"If this war mushrooms into a major conflict and a hundred thousand young Americans are killed, it won't be U.S. senators who die. It will be American soldiers who are too young to qualify for the Senate."

—SENATOR GEORGE MCGOVERN

"Wars have never hurt anybody except the people who die."

—SALVADOR DALÍ

"And if my thought-dreams could be seen, they'd put my head inside a guillotine."

—BOB DYLAN

# Contents

# Foreword: Letter from Michael Pedersen

March 14, 2003

Hello,

Hey momma, well sorry I haven't been able to call. They took the phones seven days ago; and before the office at Hunter in Savannah would only dial local numbers; they wouldn't even dial 1-800 could you believe it? We are out here in the middle of the desert and they can't even dial the numbers we need. Anyway I got the letters and box. That is so cool your first grandson came the same day your oldest son did. How is everyone? I am doing fine we are just out here in the sand and wind storms waiting; what in the world is wrong with George "TRYING TO BE LIKE HIS DAD" Bush? He got us out here for nothing what so ever. I am so furious right now momma. I really hope they do not re-elect that fool honestly. I am in good spirit and I am doing ok; I really miss you guys. Thanks for the bible and books and candy. I really look forward to letters from you guys. I received 2 letters already from family in MINN. Tell them all thanks for the support. Tell all the family hello and that I am doing fine. We don't expect anything to happen anytime soon. I cannot wait to get home and get back to my life. Tell Spudnick congrads and I'll see my first nephew soon as I get back to the states. I am sorry I wasn't able to call you guys; I hope you understand. I'm sorry I had to send you that grim letter last time; I just didn't have time to discuss that type of stuff with you before I left. Next time it will be 1 of my first priorities. Hope you guys are doing ok and keep sending the mail, it makes getting through the day easier. Well I am on my way to bed so I will write you guys soon. I love and miss all you guys.

Love,
Mike

# Will They
# Ever Trust
# Us Again?

# Introduction

A man came up to me on the street the other day and introduced himself as a navy officer just back from Iraq.

"I was on a ship off the coast of Iraq the night you gave your Oscar speech" (see page 8), he began. (This is a beginning I am not all that unfamiliar with; only the location of where each individual heard the speech is different.)

"When you said what you said about the president and the war, I was really angry at you. I booed along with all the others who were booing you.

"But now that I've been over there for the better part of the last year and seen what I've seen and know what I know . . . I just want to apologize to you for being so mad at you that night."

He held out his hand, and I shook it. I then said "You do not owe me any apology. What did you do wrong? *You believed your commander in chief.* You're *supposed* to believe your commander in chief! You're in the navy! All of us should be able to believe whatever comes out of our president's mouth. If we can't have that—at the very least THAT—then what are we left with?"

I went on to tell him that just because I didn't believe Bush in that first week of the war and said so in a very public way doesn't make me right. I didn't know if I was right that night. I'm not a weapons inspector. I *thought* I was right, but, hey, I coulda been wrong. It just turns out that I was a good guesser and a bad Oscar speech giver.

"No," I said to the navy officer, "*you* don't apologize to *me*—it is *I* who needs to apologize to *you*. I and the American people owe you and all the other servicemen and women over there a HUGE apology for sending you into harm's way when it was not only *not* necessary, it was done to line the pockets of a few greedy men. To risk your life for that, I am sorry, and millions of Americans are sorry. Please forgive *us*."

I think he was a bit shocked to hear this.

"Well, hey, Mr. Moore, *you* didn't send me over there!"

"But I didn't find the right words to convince enough people. I am, in part, responsible. And I helped to pay for it. I pay my taxes, so that means I continue to foot the bill. I am responsible."

We chatted a bit longer and then I wished him well. He asked for my email address. I told him to send me a letter, that I like getting letters from our troops.

Truth is, I get thousands of them. In the weeks and months since that night of the Oscars my email box has been flooded with letters from soldiers in Iraq and Afghanistan. At first I was surprised. I guess I made the wrong assumption that guys in the military were not going to be very supportive of what I had to say about the man in the Oval Office and my desire to prevent him from taking us to war.

But, as I found out, that was far from the truth. Letter after letter from these soldiers expressed a profound disillusionment with our mission in southwest Asia. What makes their comments unique and so intense is the fact that they are not the words of the Left or the rhetoric of the antiwar movement—they *are* the war movement. Their observations are filled with such purpose because they are the *witnesses* to war, the men and women on the ground being asked to do the killing and slowly realizing that their job has little to do with defending the United States of America.

Since the beginning of the war the American media has worked overtime to portray our brave troops as some sort of monolithic machine of men who are of one mind to rid Iraq of the bad guys and bring the goodness of Uncle Sam to that country. It wasn't until *Fahrenheit 9/11* that most people had any clue there were so many soldiers NOT in support of what Bush was doing. I was amazed at screenings of the film, watching people with their jaws open, as soldier after soldier spoke of his dissatisfaction with the war effort. Why had we not heard these voices before? Surely the media knew this was a growing feeling among the troops. Those networks are there in Iraq every damn day—I've never set foot in the country! How could I find this out so easily—and they couldn't?

Of course the answer is they've known all along that this is how many of the troops feel about the war. They knew and they covered it up. Just as they did with so many other things about this war and the "reasons" why we went to war. Covered it up or looked the other way. Censored themselves so that others higher up wouldn't have to. It has been nothing short of disgraceful and dishonest that our free press first refused to do its job—ask the hard questions and demand the evidence before letting a president take us to war—and then went on to paint a picture of troop morale in Iraq that simply has no bearing in truth.

Just the fact that this book needs to be published should be an embarrassment to our national mainstream media. If they had reported on what you are about to read in this book, these letters would never have had to be sent and I would not have to waste good paper in bringing them to you.

Now, talk like this will only get me in trouble with these so-called journalists. Their "conventional wisdom" (which is usually so full of b.s. and nearly always wrong that it pains me to denigrate the word *wisdom* when used in this way) is that people like Michael Moore and his ilk are despised by the troops because they don't support the troops and their antiwar work undermines the war effort and puts these young men and women in even more danger.

But then along comes an article like the one in the *Washington Observer-Reporter* from Pennsylvania about the veteran who had set up a "cyberspace bookmobile" on the Internet to get free books to our soldiers in Iraq. It's called BooksForSoldiers.com. You probably haven't heard of it as not one other paper picked it up—perhaps because it contains a paragraph that flies in the face of everything the media hold sacred about the Michael Moore they've invented:

> The most popular fiction request: anything by Stephen King, Williams said, with Tom Clancy a close second. It might surprise some people to learn that filmmaker and vocal Bush critic Michael Moore is the most popular non-fiction request, but Williams confirms that's the case.

When I read that, I have to admit, even I was surprised. But why should I be? Remember when the war started and how kind of scary it was to make any statement against the war? If you did, you had better follow it up immediately with this line: "BUT I SUPPORT THE TROOPS!!"

I am here to tell you that you didn't need to say that. Of course you support the troops! Who are "the troops"? The majority of them come from the poor and working classes, the very people most of you have always sided with. Many of you have spent your lives helping those who sooner or later become "our troops." At the very least, most of you have voted for representatives who have promised to be the advocates for those who grow up on the other side of the tracks. You do not need to be defensive and blurt out that you support the troops. As far as I'm concerned, that's all we have ever done.

And the troops know it. That's why they want my books and that's why when I asked them if I could share their letters with you, they were ecstatic. The chance that someone might listen to them, that their voices would be heard by millions, moved them deeply. Not one soldier whom I asked to contribute his or her letter to this book refused.

As I am writing this, I am at my father's home in Michigan. He turned eighty-three today. I am so proud of my dad. He served in the First Marine Division all through the worst battles of the South Pacific in World War II. His brother, Lornie, was killed in the Philippines. He told me tonight that I reminded him of his brother and how much he wishes we kids could have gotten to know him.

My dad never talked about the war much while we were growing up. He told us that if we heard anyone talking a lot about his war stories, he was probably never really in combat because if you were in combat you never wanted to relive it, only forget it. My dad has always been a peaceful and gentle man, and I have benefited much in having the good fortune of being his son.

He still loves the Marines, still has some Marine stuff around the house, but as he watched the news tonight, with Mr. Bush refusing to condemn the ads which smeared John Kerry and his service to our country, my dad was filled with disgust. And then on TV came fellow World War II vet Bob Dole claiming that "Kerry never bled," even though he had three purple hearts. My dad was nothing short of offended.

"Bush didn't even show up for his service—and he thinks he has the right to do this to Kerry?" he asked incredulously. "Let's hope Bush doesn't win."

By the time you are reading this Bush may or may not have won. Regardless of the outcome of the 2004 election, the Iraq War does not seem as if it will be over any time soon. I hope that the letters in this book will provide some glimpse into what many soldiers are feeling about the "mission" on which they've been sent.

A few words about the ground rules in this book: In asking these soldiers for their permission to reprint their letters to me, I gave them the option of remaining anonymous. A lot of what they have written can and will get them into trouble. That is not something I want to see happen. So I encouraged their anonymity. Nonetheless, many of the soldiers wanted their names to be printed. All I can say to the Pentagon is that I ask you, in the spirit of everything this country stands for—and especially that First Amendment, which guarantees everyone freedom of expression— not to harm these good soldiers who have risked their lives for us and who have courageously chosen to let their fellow Americans in on what they have personally seen. There is no reason to punish them for speaking the truth. They have not disobeyed your orders. They have shown up and done their job (unlike a certain man who now sits in our White House). Leave them alone. If you don't, I will do everything I can to shine a very public light on any of your vengeful actions and I will provide whatever help I can to any of these soldiers whom you may try to punish.

Near the end of this book, I have included two other chapters of letters. One batch is letters from the family and friends of soldiers in Iraq and Afghanistan. So many families have had to suffer at home through this ordeal. Whether it's been the attempts by the Bush administration to cut aid to soldiers' families or to cut back on their combat pay or to reduce services to veterans, it's clear that there is one group of people in this country who don't support our troops and it's called the Bush White House. Again, another story untold by the media.

The other is a group of letters from veterans of past wars. I wanted to give voice to these older Americans who learned the lessons of war long ago and have much to offer our young soldiers today.

We are now learning of the multitudes of soldiers who, after returning home, have found that they don't have jobs and that their lives are in ruins. Some are suicidal. They need our help. The ones who have returned home without limbs or eyes—and they number in the thousands—also need our assistance. In the back of the book I have listed resources for you to help them. There is also a list of ways to help the people of Iraq who have been ravaged by our war. And there are some ideas about what you can personally do to help end the war.

Earlier last winter, I went to the home of Lila Lipscomb in Flint, Michigan. She lost her son in Karbala, Iraq. She wanted to know if she could read me his last letter home. We rolled film. Sitting behind the camera, I tried to control my tears. I didn't want her to see me crying. But the pain caused by this man's last words rang loud inside my head (as it will to my dying day). I thought I was going to have to stop filming because I couldn't see through the tears any longer. Then she got to a line in his letter, a line that was, in effect, his last wish: "what in the world is wrong with George 'TRYING TO BE LIKE HIS DAD' Bush? He got us out here for nothing what so ever. I am so furious right now momma. I really hope they do not re-elect that fool honestly."

I stopped crying. From the grave, SGT Michael Pedersen, the son of Lila Lipscomb, was asking a nation to do one last thing for him, a young man who gave up his life for us. Is this not the least we can do? In that moment I knew what I would do for the rest of 2004—honor Michael Pedersen's request from his last letter home.

My hope, as I write this, is that all of you who support the troops will join me in doing what SGT Pedersen has asked us to do.

Michael Moore
Flint, Michigan
August 23, 2004

Transcript of Michael Moore's Oscar Award acceptance speech:

"Thank you. Thank you very much. Ahh. On behalf of our producers, Kathleen Glynn, and Michael Donovan from Canada, I'd like to thank the Academy for this. I have invited my fellow documentary nominees on the stage with us, and we would like to, they are here, they are here in solidarity with me because we like nonfiction. We like nonfiction and we live in fictitious times. We live in the time where we have fictitious election results that elects a fictitious president. We, we live in a time where we have a man sending us to war for fictitious reasons. Whether it's the fiction of duct tape or the fiction of orange alerts, we are against this war, Mr. Bush. Shame on you, Mr. Bush. Shame on you. And any time you got the pope and the Dixie Chicks against you, your time is up. Thank you very much."

# Part I

# Letters
# from Iraq

(currently in Iraq,
already served
in Iraq, or
on their way)

## "Is Everyone Blind?"

FROM: Anonymous
SENT: Friday, July 9, 2004 11:19 AM
TO: mike@michaelmoore.com
SUBJECT: You are a true patriot

Hi Mike,

I am a U.S. army sergeant stationed in Camp Warhorse Baqubah in Iraq. I saw your movie yesterday, and it gives me hope for our country. It only takes one good man to stand up for what is right to build confidence. I often asked myself the following questions: Where is our country heading? Is everyone blind? When will someone speak the truth? But finally your movie revives my spirit. All my battle buddies keep asking: What are we doing here? Why are we here?

Two days ago one of my best friends lost both of his legs after an improvised explosive device (IED) hit his convoy. He got married right before he was deployed and did not even have time for a honeymoon. We are all sad after seeing him, and we all started asking ourselves again: How many more have to die? How many more have to lose limbs before we get out of this place?

Now when we get angry, your movie will be our therapy. We thank you for what you did, and I encourage you to keep investigating 'cause there is a lot more that needs to be said. Who knows, maybe there will be a *Fahrenheit 9/11 #2!* I will keep my name confidential for safety.

## "War Slaves"

From: Al Lorentz
Sent: Saturday, May 22, 2004 10:32 AM
To: mike@michaelmoore.com
Subject: An old soldier in combat thanks you

*They serve so that we don't have to. They offer to give up their lives so that we can be free. It is, remarkably, their gift to us. And all they ask for in return is that we never send them into harm's way unless it is absolutely necessary. Will they ever trust us again?*

Dear Mr. Moore,

Thank you for these words. I am an old soldier, serving in combat in Iraq. Thank you and people like you for seeing that these wonderful kids who serve in the military aren't just war slaves to be sent mindlessly into needless wars at the whim of the foolish. Every one of us in the military swears an oath to uphold and defend the Constitution of the United States. This war has nothing to do with upholding and defending that Constitution.

The military is for defending the republic; it is not for overthrowing dictators, building "democracy," or making the world a better place for everyone else. While these may, at times, be noble goals, it cannot be the business of a free and democratic society, or else it will cease to be a republic and become an empire.

I pray that we will hold this administration accountable and that we teach all our politicians that they are not our lords and masters but are in fact public servants and that NONE of them is above the law but rather are subject to it.

## "Chicken Hawks on Patrol"

From: Ted Fattel
Sent: Tuesday, May 11, 2004 2:27 PM
To: mike@michaelmoore.com
Subject: Iraq

Dear Mike,

I wanted to tell you to keep up the fight against all the raging stupidity that seems to be going on back home. I just saw on your site where Rush Limbaugh thought this prisoner abuse was some sort of prank. OK, sure. Does he have any idea that the release of all this only makes the lives of the guys on the ground harder? That the guys out there who hate us probably hate us more now?

But then again, those pompous fools have never been in a place where being mortared is a daily occurrence. Where hearing (and feeling) explosions is something that you just get used to. I'm sure Sean Hannity and Limbaugh have never heard the BOOOM and prayed to God that one of their friends didn't just buy it. Let the chicken hawks come on over here and do a patrol or two, then watch their attitudes change.

I'll keep checking your website as long as I have Internet capability. I've read your books, and aside from endorsing Oprah for president (my wife would never let me hear the end of it), I am in FULL agreement with you.

## "Sinking Feeling"

From: Rick Bauer
Sent: Saturday, April 17, 2004 5:00 PM
To: mike@michaelmoore.com
Subject: The situation in the Gulf

Dear Mr. Moore,

I am stationed out here in the Gulf. Many of us came out here as volunteers in the wake of the threat from al Qaeda. We were proud to do our part for America, and for the safety of the world. None of us could ever believe, let alone imagine, that the War Powers order, which legally binds us to our original mission, would be subverted into a Hydra of monstrous proportions.

I was sent out here two years ago as part of the war effort in Afghanistan. But when the war drums started sounding for Iraq, I can't tell you the sinking feeling many of us felt here. We watched helplessly as the moral high ground and broad-based support we arrived with following 9/11 evaporated almost overnight.

Many of us hoped that it was simply brinkmanship by the Bush administration, to make Saddam comply with inspections. And we hoped that Congress would keep the situation in check, and prevent any authorization of an actual (yet alone expanded) Iraqi war effort. I can't adequately describe to you the huge wave of depression when the powers that be committed us to the madness we have now inherited.

While the Gulf states universally despised Saddam and his sons, the Iraq invasion was almost universally viewed as a grudge match between the Bushes and the Husseins. The fact that the Iraqi people would have to suffer untold casualties, in order to settle this long-standing blood feud, continues to fuel resentment among local Arabs. Bush has unleashed on Western society a maelstrom, which has quickly engulfed us, and which we (and our children) will have to struggle with for decades to come. All the best to you and your family.

## "I'VE SEEN MANY FRIENDS DIE OR LOSE LIMBS"

FROM: Django
SENT: Thursday, May 27, 2004 3:07 PM
TO: mike@michaelmoore.com
SUBJECT: A soldier in Iraq

Dear Mike,

Hi, I'm a soldier serving in the army in Iraq. I've been here over a year and have seen many friends and fellow soldiers die or lose limbs. I have some reservations about writing to you because of the regulations about talking negatively about the president, but then there is the issue that I don't see him as the real president. He doesn't represent the majority of the nation and certainly has never been in our shoes (soldiers at war, the working class, literate people, etc.).

I am writing to tell you and anyone else who may read this that it is people like you and others who are outspoken about the government who are the real patriots. I wish George W. Bush no harm, but I will continue to fulfill my obligations to the oath I took. To defend the country and the Constitution from enemies foreign and domestic.

I, and many other soldiers along with me, deeply appreciate the support from the citizens of the nation. I just wish I was able to defend the country and not be a pawn in this war for political agendas. We will give our lives to protect our fellow soldiers, but I have yet to defend the country from an enemy that was actually a threat to the nation.

I can't wait until the Iraqis over here make an illegal bootleg copy of *Fahrenheit 9/11* so we can see it. I think it is important for all of the acts of this administration to get out before we have another election disaster.

## "Come and Die for Us!"

From: Kyle Waldman
Sent: Friday, February 27, 2004 2:35 AM
To: mike@michaelmoore.com
Subject: None

Michael Moore,

I have been living in a world of contradictions between my commitment as a service member and being true to my morals and values. I should explain first why I chose to enlist in the army.

I was a naive 19-year-old looking for a different route in life. Like most enlisted soldiers, we signed our lives away before actually going through a self-scrutinizing process to help us learn what a demanding commitment it was. We certainly did not know what it meant to be a soldier, but we were going to find out soon enough.

When a prospective enlistee arrives at the recruiter's station, the thing that lured us in was not a poster saying, "Come and die for us, even if it means that that action may go against everything you believe in." It was, "Get your $35,000 for college!" As most people know, recruiters aren't the most honest people, but they sure do have a wonderful sales pitch! Now my naïveté does not excuse my actions, but in this case it has many consequences. For me, the consequence is finishing the contract I signed up for. However, I had no idea my commander in chief was going to create all these blasphemies.

When war was first declared, America seemed to dehumanize the Iraqi people, making them all enemies. A perfect example of this was using AAFES (equivalent to a Wal-Mart) as a propaganda machine printing off T-shirts and coffee mugs poking fun of Iraq

17

and its people. My time in Iraq has taught me a little about the Iraqi people and the state of this war-torn, poverty-stricken country.

The illiteracy rate in this country is phenomenal; most civilians have completed a fifth-grade education level. There are a couple of families I did some humanitarian relief for who lived under the roof of these two houses, and they are the ones who suffer the most in times of war, especially when the ends were totally unnecessary.

There were some farmers who didn't even know there was a Desert Storm or OIF. This was when I realized that this war was initiated by the few who would profit from it and not for its people. We, as the Coalition Forces, did not liberate these people; we drove them even deeper into poverty. I don't foresee any economic relief coming soon to these people by the way Bush has already diverted its oil revenues to make sure there will be enough oil for our SUVs.

As we can all obviously see, Iraq was not and is not an imminent threat to the United States or the rest of the world. Most of the terrorists are foreigners coming into Iraq to rebel against the Coalition Forces. However, I do believe Saddam Hussein should have been removed from power, but we certainly did not exhaust every possible means. I have also heard that Bush banned media coverage of the body bags arriving to the United States, and that was a brilliant logistical move made just in time to not jeopardize Bush's coming election.

No matter what the latest CNN or Pentagon polls say on troop morale, in all honesty, with the constant stop loss and extensions, the U.S. military will experience a shortage in the years to come because of the way our leaders have conducted themselves. A while back some military officials announced that they do not need any more troops to deploy in theater, and yet they turn around and extend units for another six months on top of the twelve months already served. Was the announcement saying they didn't need more soldiers a scheme to portray to the public that we have things under control when we, in actuality, do not?

We are here trying to keep peace when all we have been trained for is to destroy. How are two hundred thousand soldiers supposed to take control of this country? Why didn't we have an effective plan to rebuild Iraq's infrastructure? Why aren't the American people more aware of these atrocities? From the national deficit to destroying thirty years' work of environmentalists to this war, why is Bush still in power? My fiancée and I have seriously looked into moving to Canada as political refugees.

This was a bit more than I originally anticipated, but I hope I got the message across. I want to thank you for creating an interactive website where soldiers are able to express themselves freely. You definitely earned some "cool points" from me.

## "OPERATION BAN CENSORSHIP"

FROM: Michael W.
SENT: Tuesday, July 13, 2004 12:28 PM
TO: mike@michaelmoore.com
SUBJECT: Dude, Iraq sucks

My name is Michael W. and I am a 30-year-old National Guard infantryman serving in southeast Baghdad. I have been in Iraq since March of '04 and will continue to serve here until March of '05.

I was just home to Seattle for a fifteen-day R&R, and while I was home I just had to see *Fahrenheit 9/11*. My wife and I saw it together, and I have to tell you we were so disgusted we almost had to leave the theater.

Not because we didn't like the movie or disagreed with the film, but because of the hard truths of our administration's dealings in Iraq and the way the soldiers—soldiers like me—are being used to enforce W's personal agenda, and are killing and being killed for it. I am embarrassed to be a part of it!

While in Iraq I have had some heated debates over our involvement in the war. Some of my more right-wing "blind-follower" soldier buddies (and trust me, there are a lot of them) have said to me on more than one occasion, "You signed up, you have to deal with it," or "He [W.] is our commander, and you should just go along with the program."

My response is BULLSHIT! Yes, I signed a contract with the government to serve in our military, and proudly, but I never thought that our military would be used in such a self-serving, crooked, and disgraceful way. Nowhere does my contract say that I should put my life on the line for a handful of select socialite

ELITES. My contract says that I must protect and defend the Constitution of the United States!

So in that respect, it would make much more sense to be activated in support of "Operation Ban Censorship" or "Operation End Discrimination." However, something tells me there is no money in doing the right thing for the greater good, so I can expect that those "operations" are not high on the list of potential "targets."

In the few short months my unit has been in Iraq, we have already lost one man and have had many injured (including me) in combat operations. And for what? At the very least, the government could have made sure that each of our vehicles had the proper armament to protect us soldiers.

In the early morning hours of May 10th, one month to the day from my 30th birthday, I and twelve other men were attacked in a well-executed roadside ambush in southeast Baghdad. We were attacked with small-arms fire, a rocket-propelled grenade, and two well-placed roadside bombs. These roadside bombs nearly destroyed one of our Hummers and riddled my friends with shrapnel, almost killing them.

They would not have had a scratch if they had the "Up Armour" kits on them. So where was W. on that one? Turns out we finally got some of the kits, and the funny thing is we have had zero engagements with the "enemy" since that night. Go figure, maybe too little too late?

It's just so ridiculous, which leads me to my next point. A Blackwater contractor makes $15,000 a month for doing the same job as my pals and me. I make about $4,000 a month over here. What's up with that?

Beyond that, the government is calling up more and more troops from the Reserves. For what? Man, there is a huge fucking scam going on here! There are civilian contractors crawling all over this country. Blackwater, Kellogg Brown and Root, Halliburton, on and on. These contractors are doing everything you can think of from security to catering lunch!

Christ, I'm sure my father would have loved some great, catered lunch at the all night chow hall during his time in Vietnam. We are spending money out the ass for this shit, and very few of the projects are going to the Iraqi people. Someone's back is getting scratched here, and it ain't the Iraqis'!

Whatever happened to the Marshall Plan? Surely some general could blow the dust off that file and get something good going for this country and its people! Right? The fact that we don't shows me that the administration has no interest in really making a difference here or they would have already gotten the Marshall Plan out and put it to work. It's a great plan that worked during World War II when our government demonstrated its desire to get Germany and Japan back on track after causing way more destruction and disruption than even dreamed of in Iraq. The administration is so obviously capable of being successful here. Christ, there is a template already made for them.

Along with this, you have no idea how much time we sit on our asses vs. being involved in any real "fighting." Yet W. is making the case for a buildup to gain control of the country. What for? We control everything already, and some units here do nothing but sit on their asses! YES, there is fighting in Iraq; YES there is combat. But some folks ain't seeing it, so why call more damn troops? Why disrupt more lives when there are more than enough resources already here to take care of all of this nonsense? EASY FIX: Send the units sitting on their butts to the places that need more troops! Surely the generals know some folks are not doing a damn thing over here! They are in charge, right?

Or is it that W. wants to portray some big conflict that is spinning out of control to warrant more troops, to warrant more contractors, ultimately warranting leaving him in place in the upcoming election? These guys are making bank off this bullshit war, and us soldiers are paying in more ways than one! When the war is over, what is next for me? I have no clue. My life is left to chance at this point. I just hope I come home alive.

## "President Doesn't Care"

From: Specialist Willy
Sent: Tuesday, March 9, 2004 1:23 PM
To: mike@michaelmoore.com
Subject: Thank you

Mike,

I'd like to thank you for all of the support you're showing for the soldiers here in Iraq. I am in Baghdad right now, and it's such a relief to know that people still care about the lemmings who are forced to fight in this conflict.

I spoke to you when you visited the Borders on State Street in Chicago, and told you I had two weeks before I left for the war. It reminded me of that scene in *Bowling* when you were talking to Marilyn Manson and he said that instead of talking to the students from Columbine he would listen, because that's what no one ever did. Although thousands of people were waiting to see you, you listened with more concern than most of my friends did. It put me at peace.

It's hard listening to my platoon sergeant saying, "If you decide you want to kill a civilian that looks threatening, shoot him. I'd rather fill out paperwork than get one of my soldiers killed by some raghead."

We are taught that if someone even looks threatening we should do something before they do something to us. I wasn't brought up in fear like that, and it's going to take some getting used to. It's also very hard talking to people here about this war. They don't like to hear that the reason they are being torn away from their families is bullshit, or that their "president" doesn't care about them. I don't care what kind of facts you give them, they'd rather justify the war with ignorance. A few people here have become quite upset with me, and at one point I was going to be discharged for constantly inciting arguments and disrespect to my commander in chief (Dubya). It's very hard to be silenced about this when I see the same 150 people every day just going through the motions, not sure why they are doing it.

I remember talking to my dad about a possible discharge, and I remember him saying, "I know what's going to happen when you get home. You are going to turn into a bitter anti-American who hates the government, just like Michael Moore."

He knows how much I respect your work and knows you are the reason I chose to study documentary filmmaking at Columbia College in Chicago. The fact that this is the way some people see you blows my mind, and what my father said hurt me. Working as an editor for a newspaper, he is usually independent in political views. I told him to go to my apartment and take my copy of *Bowling for Columbine*. He could keep it.

As far as I am concerned, you're much more of an American than some of the people here who don't even know the reason they are fighting. I will write again, if anything interesting happens. Peace.

NOTE: *Willy sent an update in early August:* Since I first wrote, there have been about a hundred bootleg copies of *Fahrenheit* sold at my base. It is a big hit, and we are planning on playing it at our MWR [Morale, Welfare, and Recreation]. People's perceptions of this war have done a complete 180 since we got here. We had someone die in a mortar attack the first week, and ever since then, things have changed completely. Soldiers are calling their families urging them to support John Kerry. If this is happening elsewhere, it looks as if the overseas military vote that Bush is used to won't be there this time around.

## "I HATE MY COMMANDER IN CHIEF"

FROM: Anonymous
SENT: Thursday, July 29, 2004 4:51 AM
TO: mike@michaelmoore.com
SUBJECT: No time to grieve, deploy!

Hello Michael,

I'm a 20-year-old female airman currently deployed in Baghdad. I have just recently seen your movie, and I must say it moved me. I have never been interested in politics. I believe this country was founded by thieves and run by crooks, but that's neither here nor there. I've never voted, but after seeing your movie I was immediately on the Net trying to find registration papers so that when the time comes, I'll be ready.

Your movie should be rated a horror film because I was (am) horrified. I find myself stuck now because if you had made this film a year and two months earlier (my time in the service), I would NOT be in the military!

Now, I have three years to serve under a man who has never served himself before, whose whole election was a lie, and who, unfortunately, doesn't give a shit whether I live or die. It's scary to think (to know) that the president is involved in so much scandal, and nothing seems to be getting done about it.

The reason for my letter (and the meaning behind my subject line) is that about two weeks before my deployment my brother passed away (nonmilitary). Being a young airman I wasn't sure what the procedure was to take emergency leave. I was given a week. A week to grieve with my family that I hadn't seen in almost a year. And a week to say good-bye to my brother forever. As soon as I came back, with a few days of out processing, I was on my way to Baghdad. Now I'm here, and I have added stress with trying to stay focused on the mission. It hurts to know that the mission, a war that isn't even a war but a "I gotta cover up all my shit scheme" for the president, is more important than me and my family at a time of remorse.

I didn't include my name, and this is why: I hate my commander in chief. I hate the very ground he walks on, and I pray (and I know I shouldn't) that he burns in hell for what he is doing to our country and the lives of soldiers and airmen and the lives of the innocent Iraqis. Now, for three years I can look forward to serving my country with a heavy heart. I will no longer be proud to salute the flag, and I couldn't care less when the "Star-Spangled Banner" plays. I will always have respect for those who have laid down their lives for us. But right now I hate everything the flag stands for because America put this asshole in office and now half of America still thinks he is the same man they thought he was. As an African American, I ask, "Why the hell couldn't y'all just leave us be? Now we're in this bullshit with you."

I thank you for this documentary. I thank you for opening my eyes and the eyes of a lot of soldiers. I thank you for uncovering the truth that everybody knew all along but were too chicken shit to speak on. You are the man and though I may never meet you and you may never print this letter, know that you have definitely changed the life of at least one Airman.

## "GREED AND ABUSE"

FROM: Anonymous
SENT: Thursday, April 15, 2004 12:41 AM
TO: mike@michaelmoore.com
SUBJECT: From KBR truck driver now in Iraq

Mike,

I am a truck driver for KBR right now in Iraq. I will make this short because we have a time limit on using the Internet. Shortly after I got here, we were given memos from our supervisors disputing different claims in the media about KBR scandals. One memo was about an investigation by two congressmen and I had to laugh because what they are accusing is only the TIP OF A HUGE, GIGANTIC ICEBERG.

Let me give you this one small fact because I am right here at the heart of it: Since I started this job several months ago, 100% (that's right, not 99%) of the workers I am aware of are inflating the hours they claim on their time sheets. There is so much more I could tell you. But the fact is that MILLIONS AND MILLIONS of dollars are being raped from both the American taxpayers and the Iraqi people because of the unbelievable amount of greed and abuse over here. And yes, my conscience does bother me because I am participating in this rip-off.

## "I Pray My Family Does Not Have to Witness That"

From: Brad Hastings
Sent: Saturday, July 17, 2004 4:17 PM
To: mike@michaelmoore.com
Subject: I am a soldier in Baghdad

Hello, my name is Brad and I am stationed in Baghdad. I must confess that I saw your movie on bootleg DVD. Sorry. I will go home and, when it is out on DVD, pay the $15 you are entitled to for such a powerful movie.

I grew up as a Republican, but I will not be voting for Bush, that is for sure. One of the last things my father told me a few months before he passed away was that we are going to witness one of the most corrupt and brutal presidents America has ever seen. That stuck with me even before I came to Iraq. I have never been so disappointed in someone.

The movie affected me so much that I have spent all of my off time looking at some facts online, and every day I see things Bush has done that I have to go outside and take long cigarette breaks. I call my wife and vent to her. It sucks because she suffers more than me because she has to hear me vent so much that we hardly ever get a chance to talk about anything else.

It was extremely powerful to see the family who lost their son (I do pray for them, and my heart really goes out to them and all the families), and it really hit home, and I pray that my family does not have to witness that. I mean, I am prepared to die, but I am not prepared to make my family suffer for me.

I agree with freeing the people of Iraq from Saddam. I mean, he has killed many Iraqis, and from the Iraqis I have talked to, they are glad America is here. I guess that is what helps me get through the day, knowing I am hopefully doing some good.

I will not be reenlisting. I only hope that I will not get called back to this hellhole (whenever it is I get home). Anyway, I just wanted to say thank-you for the movie and hopefully it will keep Bush out of office.

## "Freedom to a Haggard Nation"

From: Jenny
Sent: Saturday, December 20, 2003 6:32 AM
To: mike@michaelmoore.com
Subject: Killing time in Baghdad

Dear Mr. Moore,

My name is Jenny; I am 26 and a specialist in the United States Army. I thank you for what you are doing for the troops with your movie. I don't think people can even begin to comprehend what a letter or a care package can mean to someone over here.

My team and I have been deployed since March 8, and in Iraq since April 1st (yes, I crossed the border on April Fools' Day). We have slept in 120-degree heat without AC, had our slumber interrupted by NBC alarms, woken up shrouded in sand day after day from the sandstorms, gone days without a shower, shit in fly-infested makeshift Porta-Johns, and burned the shit later in the day for sanitation purposes.

I have basically given up all creature comforts and freedoms that I knew, to give freedom to a haggard nation. None of what we had been through seemed to matter that first day mail arrived. A taste of home, a letter from a school, a board game to kill some time, some personal-hygiene items so that you can finally feel somewhat clean.

There comes a point out here where there is just nothing left to do, and you have nothing to look forward to. You don't know when you are going home; you lose track of the days. It's kind of like the outside world no longer matters. That is until you get mail. That is something to look forward to every couple of days. Thank you for what you do, and for informing the public about how to go about helping. If I'm not too late could you please send a copy of *Dude, Where's My Country?* I will make sure it stays in Iraq to help others after me kill time.

## "A 'FOOT SOLDIER' IN THE 'WAR ON TERROR'"

FROM: Andrew Balthazor
SENT: Friday, August 27, 2004 1:53 PM
TO: mike@michaelmoore.com
SUBJECT: Iraqi war vet—makes me sound so old

Mr. Moore,

I am an ex–Military Intelligence officer who served 10 months in Baghdad; I was the senior intelligence officer for the area of Baghdad that included the UN HQ and Sadr City.

Since Bush exposed my person and my friends, peers, and subordinates to unnecessary danger in a war apparently designed to generate income for a select few in the upper echelon of America I have become wholeheartedly anti-Bush, to the chagrin of much of my pro-Republican family. I very much appreciated your movie *Fahrenheit 9/11*, your publications, and your persistence in attempting to de-throne Bush from his place of power.

I fail to understand how Bush can be so strong regarding national security matters. As a "foot soldier" in the "war on terror" I can personally testify that Bush's administration has failed to effectively fight terrorists or the root causes of terror. A lot of people have already discussed the faulty reasoning for going to war, but even within the execution of the war, there are significant failures by the national leadership to execute the "war" on Iraq and to "reconstruct" Iraq.

For instance:

1. Bush stated that our troops would have everything we would need to fight in Iraq. Why then was I given only 19 rounds of 9mm ammunition for my only weapon, a pistol, when I crossed the border into Iraq on April 8th, 2003? Why did

hundreds of soldiers in my unit not have armor inserts for their body armor? Why did we have to use "creative accounting" to come up with cash to pay Iraqi sources for information—sometimes even using our personal funds? When we needed cell phones for Iraqi sources so they could contact us without putting themselves in danger, why were they unavailable? (Perhaps because every other person within the highly ineffective CPA [Coalition Provisional Authority] had one?)

2. The White House and the DoD failed to plan for reconstruction of Iraq. Contracts weren't tendered until Feb-Mar of 2003, and the Office of Reconstruction and Humanitarian Assistance (the original CPA) didn't even come into existence until January 2003. This failure to plan for the "peace" is a direct cause for the insecurity of Iraq today.

Immediately after the "war" portion of the fighting (which really ended around April 9th, 2003) we should have been prepared to send in a massive reconstruction effort. Right away we needed engineers to diagnose problems, we needed contractors repairing problems, we needed immediate food, water, shelter, and fuel for the Iraqi people, and we needed more security for all of this to work—which we did not have because we did not have enough troops on the ground, and CPA decided to disband the Iraqi Army. The former Iraqi police were engaged far too late; a plan should have existed to bring them into the fold right away.

Unemployment is also a contributing factor to the lack of security, since idle hands are dangerous when those hands belong to people who are hungry, thirsty, and armed. The fact that Iraq was mostly a socialized industrial economy within its cities was known. Why then was the employment of urban Iraqis during reconstruction not a priority?

3. Contractors hired by the national decision makers (no bid

contractors) contributed to problems in Iraq, instead of helping. They did this by driving out or discouraging some international and non-U.S. NGOs who were working the same areas that contractors like Bechtel were hired to fix. When areas were being double-tapped, CPA would instruct the NGOs to go away and let the contractors work. Additionally, the sub-contractors employed by U.S. contractors hired Iraqis—but they found Iraqis in rural areas outside of urban areas (to reduce the amount they would have to pay them—urban areas have a higher average daily pay), and then bring the rural Iraqis into urban areas to conduct work. This resulted in a lot of irritated, unemployed Iraqis in areas where they could see work being done, but no work (and no pay) for them. And the rub of all this is that the rural Iraqis didn't really need the work—most rural Iraqis were subsistence farmers, with a loose barter economy in the undeveloped areas outside of cities.

4. CPA was as much our enemy over there as the people planting roadside bombs and shooting weapons at us. Several times they put U.S. profit or CPA control as more important than security for either Iraqis or the U.S. troops over there. CPA was mostly staffed by young Republicans who want to put CPA/Iraq on their resume so they won't be left out of the Party.

One example of this: In late May 2003, CPA had designated a Sunni to be governor of Najaf, which was militarily under the control of a battalion of the 7th RCT of the 1st Marine Division. Najaf is The City for Shi'ites, so they didn't like this Sunni mayor. The Shi'ites protested. The Marine Battalion Commander decided to hold free elections for an interim mayor to replace the Sunni. Many different factions in Najaf put forward candidates; posters were put up all over the city, and people tried to sway the vote using street-corner speeches. The week the election was to be held the Marines had managed to rebuild a local TV station using their unit funds, and they televised the election results to the immediate area (this was the first TV station in Iraq to be operational, by the way.) This was democracy in action: the people spoke and gave their power to an elected individual. This was in late June 2003 if I remember correctly.

Several days later CPA stated the election was invalid because the Marines didn't have the authority to hold elections or change the CPA's designated mayor. What had been a victory for the U.S. and the people for Najaf had been turned sour by CPA's "don't step on our turf" mentality. By doing this, the Marines were made to appear impotent, and the Shi'ites of their Holy City lost any hope for the U.S. occupation of their land.

Is it any wonder that Sadr found an audience for his anti-American rhetoric in Najaf?

I'm sure this has gone on long enough. If there is anything I can do to help get Bush out of office, please let me know. I've left the military and am currently setting up my own business, but have time and flexibility to spare.

Andy Balthazor

## "Blessed with Common Sense"

From: Anthony Pietsch
Sent: Thursday, August 5, 2004 6:13 PM
To: mike@michaelmoore.com
Subject: Soldier for sale

Dear Mr. Moore,

My name is Tony Pietsch, and I am a national guardsman who has been stationed in Kuwait and Iraq for the past 15 months. I am fairly liberal, but I prefer to just consider myself blessed with common sense, and my opinion contrasts with many of the opinions of this brainwashed, Bush-loving society. But even though this is true, I've found that many of the people in my unit, and army wide, who have commonly voted for the Republican Party, have been changing their views about the party, especially concerning the man in charge.

I have personally worked to change the opinions of others about our fearless "commander and chief," and I've been able to take a few votes out of the hands of the villain. But I have to thank and give applause to you primarily. You have changed the minds of so many people here with *Dude, Where's My Country?* that it almost brings tears to my eyes.

As I said, I'm in Kuwait, and, stationed without a mission or purpose, we were finally called up to go and do our duty. When we arrived, we found out they didn't really have anything for us even then, so we were swept into a large group of Military Police companies that had the jobs of doing "pre-clearance customs." This is how disorganized the occupation had been. We set up shop in bases all around Kuwait and began doing customs on the Marine Corps. And other army units got set to leave the area. Our own leave date was set for Dec. 12th, but it was extended. The "one year boots on ground" order came out, and May 8th, 2004, became the new date to look forward to. In this entire time, we had been doing customs, and I've listened to the heartbreaking stories and dismal views other soldiers had on the war and its outcome.

Many soldiers I spoke to believed in the military, yet not the war. Many thought everything happened for financial gain, and they had a hard time coping with the deaths of friends and companions over such petty causes. I sympathized and tended to agree with them, though I only could understand in theory.

Along with the 1st AD and so many other guard and reserve units, my National Guard unit, the 1775th MP Company was extended due to the lack of planning and refusal to look at the complex situation that was rapidly unfolding. Finally, we were put on convoy escorts. We were on gun trucks running from the bottom of Iraq to about two hours above Baghdad.

The Iraqi resistance was insanity. I spent many nights lying awake after mortar rounds had just struck areas nearby, some coming close enough to throw rocks against my tent. I've seen roadside bombs go off all over, Iraqis trying to ram the side of our vehicle. Small children giving us the finger and throwing rocks at the soldiers in the turrets. We were once lost in Baghdad and received nothing but dirty looks and angry gestures for hours. The basic feeling around Iraq seems to be hostile. It seems the only people who try to be friendly are the people begging on the side of the road, or the poor Iraqis selling trinkets and new Iraqi currency (which they have openly proclaimed they have no faith in) outside the bases.

We made many sacrifices; I have personally been afraid for my life more days than I can count. We lost our first man only a few weeks before our tour was over, but it seems that all is for nothing because all we see is hostility and anger over our being there. They are angry over the abuse scandal and the collateral damages that are always occurring.

Here's my story: I was wooed with a contract by the recruiter at the age of 16 and as soon as I was legally able, as soon as I turned 17, I signed up, mostly because I thought it would be a good way to make a little money during high school, and because I was assured that nothing would ever happen, our country wouldn't go to war. That was July 2001. I have had only three months since I graduated and went off to basic training to be a free man.

I have gone from 18 to 20 without seeing my home. I live in constant fear, because all these laws made to protect soldiers from being overused are on the verge of being thrown out. They are constantly putting us on a stop loss, extending our time of duty. I now have to live with the fact that I can be indefinitely extended, and I have no guarantee that I will not be in a war zone the majority of the time.

Bush is constantly talking about other countries besides Iraq and Afghanistan that are security problems, and I think to myself, Is two not enough? Are you willing to just destroy my life and the lives of thousands of others on a whim? Some sort of ambitious Romanesque dream?

I don't know how the rest of my life will turn out, but I truly regret being a 16-year-old kid looking for some extra pocket money and a way to college.

## "CHOICE BECOMES CLEAR
## EVERY TIME A SOLDIER DIES"

FROM: Nicholas Fry
SENT: Sunday, July 4, 2004 8:31 PM
TO: mike@michaelmoore.com
SUBJECT: SPC Fry's last night in Iraq

Dear Mike,

My name is SPC Nicholas Fry, and I am a rifleman with the First
Armored Division. I would like to thank you for the copy of *Dude,
Where's My Country?* I read it in three days, which is fast for an
enlisted soldier who was educated by the Arizona Public School
System.

 I also recently bought a bootleg copy of your new movie
(tell your producer I apologize). I was so inspired by the book that
when my best friend's dad, who is a Vietnam vet and for some reason is a Republican, sent me an email bad-mouthing your movie, I
made an attempt at converting him. I respect and look up to this
man greatly, so this was hard for me to do. Fifteen months of pro-
Bush email will drive a person crazy.

 This is what I wrote:

Dear Mr. Tank,

I recently was sent a free copy of *Dude, Where's My Country?* from
Michael Moore and a group called Books for Soldiers. It's basically the book version of the movie *Fahrenheit 9/11*. This book
along with the bootleg copy of *Fahrenheit* I obtained in Baghdad,
do nothing to dishonor soldiers in any way. All the movie and

book do is show the financial gains of the Bush administration and the cost on the people who do their dirty work.

I would never preach to you about the loss of a comrade, as I'm sure you know it all too well from your time in Nam. I too have held the wounds of my friends and screamed "Medic" as we waited far too long for an evac. I have laughed at dead civilians and said, "Fuck 'em, they got in the way." I have collected my two grand a month while a bus driver for Halliburton makes five times what I do. I have returned from a mission covered in sweat and blood and had people that never leave the wire tell me I needed to shave. And most recently I have watched officers receive Bronze Stars even though they had not discharged their weapon ONCE. These most disgusting memories will stay with me for life as I'm sure yours do today.

I have a choice to make and that choice becomes more clear every time a soldier dies to line the pockets of rich men who will never lose sleep over the blood they have spilled.

My views may come as a shock to you, and I look up to you as a great man who served his country when it was not the most popular thing to do. I spent days wondering if I should send this email to you out of fear that you may look down on me. And I look forward to continuing this conversation upon my return in a week.

I do not consider myself a Republican or the least bit conservative and wonder how a person could. And this is why:

I do not come from a wealthy family. And I don't believe a CEO should make 200% more than his average employee and then sell his stock and buy an island where the law can't find him. I somehow fell in love with a beautiful black girl and do plan on mixing our races—sorry, John Ashcroft.

I don't believe that the government should be able to know what books I'm reading or be able to arrest me without a trial

(Patriot Act). I don't think that America should be the only Western country to put people to death as if it was God's will. I don't understand why we waste $24,000 per dopehead a year to lock up drug users when treatment is half the price. No American should be denied a trip to the doctor because he has no health insurance. It's not right to make money off of people because they are sick. And last but not least, I don't think we should be rebuilding Iraq for these fucks when we both know parts of Chandler, AZ, are just as bad.

I know this is a hell of a lot coming from a punk kid who was eating your wife's delicious meals and helping distract you while Scott stole your cigarettes only five years ago. But this is how I feel. I hope I didn't piss you off too bad, because that is not my intention. I love you and your family very much and know I am always welcome even if I am a bleeding-heart socialist LIBERAL. Hope to see you soon,

SPC Nicholas Fry B Co 2/6 Infantry, on what he prays will be his last night in Iraq.

I could not believe I had the balls to hit Send, but I did, and will continue to do it until this tyrant is out of office for good. I also brainstormed another way to help. I am gonna make it up to those hardworking producers of yours and give back some of the hard-earned American tax dollars at the same time. Upon my return to the States I will buy 100 tickets to your movie and pass them out at my local movie theater while in uniform.

Thanks again for the book and making that great film that I paid $3 to see.

## "No Way I Would End Up in Iraq"

FROM: Micah Stathis
SENT: Wednesday, July 28, 2004 11:06 PM
TO: mike@michaelmoore.com
SUBJECT: A soldier deploying to Iraq

Dear Mr. Moore,

My name is Micah Stathis and I am a specialist in the U.S. Army. I am currently in Korea, but I will be deploying to Iraq within the coming weeks. I am a Greek American, and I was, somewhat, forced to join the army. In Greece, it is mandatory for me to serve in the military for 18 months without any substantial pay. Usually, men go when they are 18; however, I was given an extension because I was in college. They called for me to serve about 18 months ago.

I was fully prepared to go. However, since I am also an American citizen, I am allowed to serve in the American military to fulfill my military obligation in Greece. After much deliberation I decided that a two-year stint in the U.S. Army was the best course of action, given the fact that I was going to get paid, and therefore able to help my mother financially. My recruiter told me that there was no way I would end up in Iraq, given the fact that Bush had announced an end to the major operations.

To make a long story short, I found out two months ago that I am going to Iraq. I have tried everything possible to get reassigned. My mother has appealed to the U.S. embassy in Greece because I am an only child; I have spoken to the chaplain about conscientious-objector status, but was refused. I have resigned myself to the fact that I am being forced into this and have no other option.

I recently saw *Fahrenheit 9/11* and I was blown away. I immediately showed it to the rest of my platoon, and I was immediately told off by an officer because I showed something that would affect morale. Everyone here is excited about going so that they can kill someone. It sickens me to listen to the way many of my fellow soldiers speak. I feel like an alien in this world, especially considering that I lean very far to the left.

I am often told by my higher-ups that we are just following orders by going to Iraq. They believe that somehow absolves us of any responsibility. The Nazis were also just following orders. I don't know how it will be in Iraq, but I will do my best to let the Iraqis know that I am completely against this occupation.

I sincerely hope that I will be able to find other soldiers in Iraq who recognize the fact that we are being used as pawns by Bush and his entourage.

## "WAR NIGHTMARES"

FROM: Craig Smith
SENT: Tuesday, July 6, 2004 6:07 PM
TO: mike@michaelmoore.com
SUBJECT: I am a soldier

Mr. Moore,

My name is Craig Smith, and I am currently an activated reservist. I volunteered to serve in Iraq when the invasion began in March of 2003.

After serving ten months in Iraq I came back to America with hopes of moving on with my life. That's when the nightmares started. I became very jumpy. You could call it being "edgy and irritable." I dealt with it for a while; then I decided that I needed help. I went to the Fort Carson Hospital to see how I could get treatment for PTSD, post-traumatic stress disorder. I was given an assessment test. My paperwork was lost by the hospital. I went again for another assessment test. This time I was seen by a doctor. During my visit with the doctor, she told me that, yes, I do have PTSD. Later, when I viewed my documentation, it said that I did not have PTSD, but that that doesn't necessarily mean that I don't suffer from it. It also stated that the treatment was complete and successful. It also stated that I have nightmares about dead children. It also stated a lot of other stuff.

Frustrated and untreated, I kept asking for help. Fort Carson gave me a number to call—a hotline. I was given a damn hotline to help me with war nightmares, Mr. Moore. I was then told that Fort Carson is understaffed and that they ONLY HAVE TWO DOCTORS ON STAFF TO HELP PTSD PATIENTS. Think about this, Michael—THOUSANDS of TROOPS returning from COMBAT and only two doctors to help them return to life! What are they doing to those who gave so much and only ask that our leaders make good decisions?

Fed up, I wrote my senator. He responded to me and is offering me help. Wayne Allard, to be exact. I thank him for his prompt response. I also went downtown in Colorado Springs to the Veterans Center to seek help from them as well. They offered me help. Everyone wants to help, Mr. Moore, except our own people.

Why is retention low? Why will no one stay in the military? Why are we fed up with duty? Not because of war, my friend. But because we are treated like un-important children. And I tell you this, no damn parade down Broadway can change that fact.

## "We Were Lied to and Used"

FROM: Sean Huze
SENT: Sunday, March 28, 2004, 7:56 PM
TO: mike@michaelmoore.com
SUBJECT: "Dude, Where's My Country?"

Mr. Moore,

I am an LCPL in the U.S. Marine Corps and veteran of Operation Iraqi Freedom. I am an infantryman and served with the 2d Light Armored Recon Battalion, attached to the 1st Marine Division from Feb 7 to May 24, 2003.

Mr. Moore, please keep pounding away at Bush. I'm not some pussy when it comes to war. However, the position we were put in—fighting an enemy that used women, children, and other civilians as shields; forcing us to choose between firing at "area targets" (nice way of saying firing into crowds) or being killed by the bastards using the crowds for cover—is indescribably horrible.

I saw more than a few dead children littering the streets in Nasiriyah, along with countless other civilians. And through all this, I held on to the belief that it had to be for some greater good. That the sacrifices we made, and the sacrifices the civilians of Iraq made, mattered. I firmly believed at the time that what we were doing was making our nation stronger.

Months have passed since I've been back home and the unfortunate conclusion I've come to is that Bush is a lying, manipulative motherfucker who cares nothing for the lives of those of us who serve in uniform. Hell, other than playing dress-up on aircraft carriers, what would he know about serving this nation in uniform?

His silence and refusal to speak under oath to the 9/11 Commission further mocks our country. The Patriot Act violates every principle we fight and die for. And all of this has been during his first term. Can you imagine his policies when he doesn't have to worry about reelection? We can't allow that to happen, and there are so many like me in the military who feel this way. We were lied to and used. And there aren't words to describe the sense of betrayal I feel as a result.

The only way to make it right is to get rid of him in November and impeach his sorry ass after he's voted out. If lying about a blow job warrants impeachment, then lying about WMD and getting thousands of people killed certainly does, too.

## "THE IRAQI PEOPLE WERE NOT FREED"

FROM: Keith Pilkington
SENT: Monday, July 5, 2004 4:08 AM
TO: mike@michaelmoore.com
SUBJECT: How I celebrated the Fourth of July

Did you celebrate the Fourth of July? Today is the Fourth of July, 2004. Every other Fourth of July was a time of joy for me. Many are preparing feasts to celebrate, but I feel like eating nothing at all. I will go to none of them. I simply have no celebratory feelings.

I'm sure some would say that I am not patriotic, and that I do not love my country. What would I say to someone if they confronted me with that accusation? I could tell them of my service in the army. I could tell them of my service in the Iraq war, the war that still rages. I don't think that would be enough. I'm no longer in the army. They would say I'm un-American and left the army out of hate for my country, and shooting fireworks is true patriotism anyway. They would say I was no patriot at all.

The same people who question my patriotism would question why I am so sad on this day of celebration. I might tell them of the Iraq War and all those that fell and will fall. They would respond by telling me all those who fell and will fall fought for the freedom of the Iraqi people. I would tell them of the great struggle to topple the tyrant, Saddam. I would tell them the Iraqi people were not freed when we toppled Saddam and are not free now.

I would tell those who question my patriotism to actually read the Declaration of Independence they celebrate so much. The Declaration of Independence states, "That to secure these rights, Governments are instituted among men, deriving their just powers from the consent of the governed." I would tell them that the Iraqi people gave no consent for the American provisional administration, but that is not my point. The American administration never secured Iraqi rights to life, liberty, and the pursuit of happiness. How many have been killed by terrorist bombings? How many innocents have died from our attacks on terrorists? How many have been the victims of crime because too few troops were there to protect them from criminals? I know. I was there.

The American administration in Iraq was not a failure. It did not secure the rights of the Iraqi people, but it did secure other things. The oil fields are secure, and American corporations secured multibillion-dollar government contracts to plunder that Iraqi oil. We should all be proud. Our right to Iraqi property is secure. Let freedom ring!

Those who question my patriotism would say that Iraq is free now. They have their own government. I would say that the Iraqis have a government instituted by the consent of the Americans and enforced by American troops, who can enter any home without any say by an Iraqi citizen. It should be Iraqi forces securing the Iraqi people's liberty. Let freedom ring!

I'm sure those who question my patriotism would have now grown quiet, their arguments against me spent. I would not take the opportunity to question their patriotism. Not everyone is as unlucky as I to have witnessed battle and have truth burned in their soul. However, I would calmly share with them the truths I have learned.

## "I Believed My President"

FROM: R.H.
SENT: Monday, July 12, 2003 4:57 PM
TO: mike@michaelmoore.com
SUBJECT: Iraqi freedom veteran supports you

Dear Mr. Moore,

I am an Operation Iraqi Freedom veteran, so *Fahrenheit 9/11* kind of hit close to home.

All my life I have pretty much been a conservative. I grew up in Elkhart, Indiana, so there were conservatives aplenty telling me how things should be the whole time I was growing up. I decided to join the military in December of 2001 while I was in college. At the time I was turning pretty liberal, not crazy, but I was moving toward the left. I wrote a paper on gun control for my sociology class. It was very radical for me at the time because I had always been Republican, conservative, and gun control was not something that I ever cared about.

Then when I joined the military, for some reason my views began to go back the other way. I was being brainwashed and lied to all because some idiot from Texas decided to act out of vengeance and hatred instead of just accepting the fact that there are people who aren't like us and that we cannot always be right.

I went to Iraq with thoughts of killing people who I thought were horrible. I was like, "Fuck Iraq, fuck these people, I hope we kill thousands." Why? I am not that kind of person. I believed my president. I thought G.W. was awesome. He was taking care of business and wasn't going to let al Qaeda push us around, or any terrorists for that matter.

I was with the 3rd Squadron, 7th Cavalry, 3rd Infantry division out of Fort Stewart, Georgia. My unit was one of the first to Baghdad and pretty much led the charge the entire way through Iraq. I was so scared. Didn't know what to think. Seeing dead bodies for the first time. People blown in half. Little kids with no legs, thanks to a few well-placed bullets. It was overwhelming, the sights, sounds, fear.

Then we started working with the people when we got to Baghdad. I thought I saw us helping them. They seemed so happy to see us, so happy that we were there. We heard during the war that the Iraqis didn't trust us because we left them during the first Gulf War and didn't help them then to get out of the shadow of Saddam. They thought we were going to leave them again.

I was over there from Jan '03 to Aug '03. I hated every minute. It was a daily battle to keep my spirits up. While I was in Iraq I read in the *Stars and Stripes* newspaper that you had received an Oscar for *Bowling for Columbine* and during the acceptance speech you bad-mouthed ole G.W. My first thought was, Wow, this guy is a shithead. I came home from Iraq and became very complacent with my life and my career. It didn't take long either.

Then a very good friend said that I should watch *Bowling for Columbine*. I was like, "No way am I going to watch a movie made by that guy." But he pretty much forced me to watch it. It was the best thing that anyone has ever done for me. My wife and I were seriously changed forever. I guess what I am trying to tell you is thank you for compelling me to be a more compassionate person and for showing me that everything is not as it seems.

I have shared my views with a lot of fellow coworkers, and the response has ranged from very harsh to very accepting. I have been called a communist, Canadian, "a person who hates this country yet milks it for all its worth," traitor, liberal faggot, tree-huggin' hippie, etc. I was called into my platoon sergeant's office after the rest of the platoon provoked me into an argument about politics, and I was told that I was not allowed to give my views anymore because we have "young impressionable soldiers who can't hear those things because it lowers morale."

I retorted by saying that I fought for the right to have my freedom of opinion. My platoon leader said that when I joined the military I gave up all my rights. My platoon sergeant called me a communist; the rest of the people in the office laughed at me, and he was making me do push-ups the whole time this was going on. I was told that if I wanted to suck dick or whatever I wanted to do, that was fine, but not to bring my views to work with me because I am not allowed to talk about George Bush badly because it didn't support my chain of command.

I hate the army and my job. I am supposed to get out next February but will now be unable to because the asshole in the White House decided that now would be a great time to put a stop loss in effect for the army. So I get to do a second tour in Iraq and be away from those I love again because some asshole has the audacity to put others' lives on the line for his personal war. I thought we were the good guys.

## "Don't Sacrifice Our Lives
## Unless Absolutely Necessary"

From: SGT, U.S. Army
Sent: Thursday, July 22, 2004 4:43 AM
To: mike@michaelmoore.com
Subject: Thank You

Dear Michael,

I just wanted to write and thank you for producing *Fahrenheit 9/11*. I was aware of many of the facts in the movie before I saw it (thanks to a book called *Sleeping with the Devil* by Robert Baer), but I'm so happy you chose to include the personal story of a military family's grief after the loss of their son.

Fortunately, and amazingly, none of my friends have died in this war. Some have been wounded, and many are deployed in hostile areas as I write this. I think it is very important that the American people understand that you can be promilitary and against the war in Iraq. I also hope that the American people know that many soldiers, like myself, are only doing their duty. My favorite line in the movie was something to the effect of: These young soldiers enlisted to protect our country and are willing to die to defend our freedom; all they ask us is to not put them in harm's way unless absolutely necessary to defend America. That phrase epitomizes how I feel about serving in the army. I am proud to serve my country, but please don't ask me or my comrades to sacrifice our lives unless absolutely necessary.

I almost didn't join the army after Bush won in 2000—that's how strongly I felt that he would be a terrible commander in chief. But $30,000 in student loan repayment and a nice bonus for a five-year commitment meant a little more to me at the time than who my new boss would be. I probably still would have joined the military knowing what I know now, but I would have done it differently. In the days after 9/11 I was never more proud to be a soldier because I thought we would be used to defend our country. In some aspects I think we have been utilized to defend our nation, but in too many instances our leaders have lost focus and we have been used inappropriately.

Your movie will hopefully affect the outcome of this presidential election. I had hoped greatly that GEN Wesley Clark would have been on the ticket somewhere, but with any luck he will be the next secretary of defense. Thank you again for all of your efforts to fire my boss. I appreciate it greatly, as do many of my colleagues who believe that patriotism is defined by the love of your country and your willingness to defend her, not by Bush's definition of: "If you aren't with us, you're against us."

## "SINGLE MOTHER"

FROM: G.G.
SENT: Saturday, July 3, 2004 11:19 PM
TO: mike@michaelmoore.com
SUBJECT: Former Marines

Hi Mike,

I saw *Fahrenheit 9/11* and I just wanted to thank you personally for letting us know the truth about what is really going on in this country. I served four years on active duty in the Marine Corps, and now I'm being told that there is a chance that I might be called back to go to Iraq and fight. I would rather sit in jail before I go and fight a war for that man who won't even fight for me and mine.

I am a single mother, and I don't understand why they are going through so much trouble to bring in reservists and retired military personnel to fight this war when there are so many other healthy people who will never be considered (i.e., the Bush twins). I do not, nor did I ever, support the war in Iraq. However, I do support our troops, and it is time to bring our troops home where they belong with their families.

## "Precious Money"

From: Anonymous
Sent: Monday, July 5, 2004 3:39 PM
To: mike@michaelmoore.com
Subject: Thank you!

Mr. Moore,

I am an army vet, and I served in Iraq for 11 months. My younger brother is a Marine and is in Iraq now. My mother, for obvious reasons, has had a very rough time for the past year and a half. She is an avid fan of yours and has seen your film at least five times. She hates the entire Bush administration, and I think that your movie helps her cope with her fear and anger.

I've been looking around on your website today, and I'm glad to see that you have links to organizations that support the troops in Iraq and encourage people to vote. Just out of curiosity, I went to the home page for the White House and to President Bush's reelection website, and I couldn't find any link to anything that really even mentioned what the troops over there are going through. It seems that they are concerned more about the Iraqi people and their precious money than they are about the welfare of the American soldiers.

## "Fictitious Reasons"

From: A Marine lieutenant
Sent: Tuesday, December 23, 2003 6:44 PM
To: mike@michaelmoore.com
Subject: Iraq

Mr. Moore,

I am an officer in the United States Marine Corps who has recently returned from Iraq after nearly six months. I bought a copy of *Dude, Where's My Country?* on a whim, and read it nonstop in about two days. The issues that you raise are ones that I have dealt with firsthand. I find it difficult to believe that there is a more Orwellian environment in the country than the military, where expressing anything other than complete adoration for Bill O'Reilly and Fox News is considered tantamount to treason.

My unit was one of the initial units to enter Iraq. Prior to the start of the war, several of my Marines (I was a platoon commander at the time, in charge of 60 Marines) came and asked me if it was true that we were going to war for oil, as many Marines were saying. This concerned me so much I called the platoon together and explained to them why we were going to war with Iraq, as I understood it.

I told them that Saddam Hussein was a vile dictator who posed a serious threat to our national security and to world peace, largely due to his possession of weapons of mass destruction. I told them we knew for sure he had them, and were going in to capture his WMD so he couldn't kill anyone with them. My Marines seemed to accept this as a good reason to risk their lives. Time and our senior leadership have proven me to be a liar; we apparently went to war for, as you put it, fictitious reasons. This angers me more than I can possibly express.

If you choose to post this email, please remove any information that might identify me. As you know, the Uniform Code of Military Justice, the laws that govern the military, make speaking contemptuously about our nation's leaders a criminal offense. I don't believe that I've done that. After all, I'm only saying they failed us (the troops), but as an officer they'd really stomp me if they thought I had. Thank you very much for your time.

## "National Emergency?"

From: Nathaniel Franco
Sent: Thursday, July 8, 2004 3:05 AM
To: mike@michaelmoore.com
Subject: IRR troop

Mr. Moore,

I am a soldier in the IRR or individual ready reserve. I was released from active duty May 25, 2004, with an honorable discharge. I participated in both Operation Enduring Freedom and Operation Iraqi Freedom and now find myself facing the possibility of having to go back again.

The main point I would like to make is that the IRR option on our contracts is only supposed to be exercised in case of a "national emergency." It says plainly on our enlistment contract. How can anyone consider insurgent attacks in a land far, far away a national emergency? After all, the MISSION ACCOMPLISHED banner was hung long ago. Mike, thanks for all you do for the troops.

*Fahrenheit 9/11* is by far the most outstanding support our troops need right now. Thank you for caring and trying to make George W. Bush and his contemporaries responsible for their villainous acts.

## "MAKE RICH IDIOTS RICHER"

FROM: SGT Alex Ward
SENT: Friday, April 16, 2004 7:29 AM
TO: mike@michaelmoore.com
SUBJECT: Greetings from SGT Ward

Hey Michael,

My name is SGT Alex Ward, USMC. I'm an Arabic linguist stationed in Fort Gordon, Georgia. I volunteered to go to Iraq, but was denied. I wanted to go to support my friends over there, not to support this idiotic war.

I spent time in Guantánamo; I was interpreting for the detainees down there. Actually, that is where I checked out your book *Stupid White Men* at the base library. I believe what we did in Afghanistan was justified, kicking out the Taliban and al Qaeda there. This Iraq thing is more than a debacle, it is a freaking abortion! It was obvious Saddam had no WMDs, that there were no al Qaeda links, and that the unholy trinity of Bush, Cheney, Rumsfeld already had their minds made up that they were going in, no matter if anything was found or not.

I'm extremely pissed that my friends are fighting and dying to make rich idiots richer, when they could actually be looking for the real terrorist, Mr. bin Laden. Iraq has been a drain on our manpower, resources and national morale, and has turned a nation that had relatively few terrorists into one swarming with them. Keep up the good work, bro!

## "CAN'T WE IMPEACH THIS JACKASS???"

FROM: Sean
SENT: Wednesday, May 5, 2004 9:41 PM
TO: mike@michaelmoore.com
SUBJECT: National Guard and scared shitless

Hello Mike,

I am writing you today because I am with the 834th Support Battalion of the Minnesota National Guard. Due to the fact that the Bush war machine needs more bodies to be put into it, we have been activated to be shipped to the front on Aug. 1 of this year. We have been told that we are to spend the next TWO years in-country! My wife is due to give birth to our son a month before I am to leave for that hell on earth.

My life is ruined if this happens. Loss of wages, medical care, and God knows what other things. TWO fucking years! My son will be walking by then, and who knows if I will even make it back at all to see my family! I hate our leaders who take part-time Guard members, who are NOT professional soldiers, and destroy their lives to make theirs more profitable. Can't we impeach this jackass???

I joined a few years ago so I could get a loan for a house. Christ, now I'm staring down the barrel of a gun my president (ha-ha!) has pointed at my head.

NOTE: *Sean and his wife had a baby, a son, in the summer of 2004. He is very healthy and active.*

## "THE DIRECTION MY COUNTRY
## IS HEADING"

FROM: Pete
SENT: Tuesday, May 4, 2004 12:45 PM
TO: mike@michaelmoore.com
SUBJECT: Letter from a veteran

Dear Mr. Moore,

I have served over five years in the army as both an enlisted member and an officer. I just got back last month (April) from Iraq. I spent 15 months over there and it was definitely crazy. In addition to the campaign medals, I also received the Bronze Star for my service. I don't regret having served my country, but I have become very frustrated with the direction my country is heading. I have decided to resign my commission, and I am moving up to Seattle to start a pizza restaurant (which also has a vegan menu) with Joe, a friend from college. Right now, we're doing the research on getting permits, taxes, etc. Hopefully with Joe being a minority and me being a vet, we will be able to get some grant money.

Anyway, after reading your book we wanted to use the principles you stated to business owners: pay your workers more, give them health benefits, and hire minorities. I suppose the reason I wanted to write you is that in case our business ever gets off the beaten track for whatever reason, and Joe and I are not living up to our own mission statement, I think I may need someone like you to show me my own letter and say, "Pete, you promised to be a good business owner. You also promised to change the direction of this country and you're not doing that!" I guess I wanted to write you so that I ensure that I never turn my back on my own ideals.

NOTE: *Pete ultimately retracted his resignation papers, deciding he should stay in the military because he felt he could make more of a difference there.*

## "IT REALLY MAKES ME WANT TO VOTE"

FROM: Vadim Nuniyants
SENT: Thursday, July 15, 2004 11:57 AM
TO: mike@michaelmoore.com
SUBJECT: From an ex-Marine—Thanks, Mike

Hi Mike,

My name is Vadim Nuniyants; I am 22 years old and I live in Renton, Washington. I have just finished watching *Fahrenheit 9/11* and wanted to thank you personally for making this film. Only about a year or two ago did I start to get more political, and that's what I loved the most about this movie. It makes the everyday Joe want to act on his opinions/beliefs. It really makes me want to vote, which I will be doing for the first time this upcoming election.

I spent three years in the Marines, up until January of 2003, when I got orders to ship out to Kuwait and Iraq. I told my commanding officer that I refused to go. I spent the next five months in New Orleans, Louisiana, where I met other Marines who refused to fight this war. The military classified us as conscientious objectors, and our commanders classified us as flag burners. The young men whom I have met in New Orleans were some of the bravest people I have come across. They would have rather gone to jail than fight in Iraq. One of my buddies down there, Stephen Funk, was actually court-martialed, and did go to the brig for six months. But I'm sure that he saw that as a small price to pay for doing what he believed in. But the funny thing is, he is the only CO I've met who had to go to jail. This is because he was the only CO who went public with his refusal to fight. He has done interviews with radio shows and newspapers.

In the end, I got an honorable discharge, which is why I urge more and more members of the military to stand up for what they believe. Stephen got discharged after serving jail time. And some Marines get denied, like my friend R.A., who refused to fight, like me, but his claim was denied and he was sent back to his unit. About a month ago his unit got activated again, and so he is back in New Orleans going through the big green process.

You know, about a year ago when I would tell someone that I refused to fight in Iraq, most people considered me unpatriotic. For me, the only unpatriotic thing I could have done would have been to go over there and fight for a cause that I knew to be false. These days more and more people are starting to see things more clearly. More and more people are forming opinions. More and more people are shedding their fears, and more and more people are growing full from being fed lies and being told what to do. People are taking control and taking responsibility.

## "WHY WERE WE THERE?"

FROM: Joseph Cherwinski
SENT: Saturday, July 3, 2004 8:33 PM
TO: mike@michaelmoore.com
SUBJECT: "Fahrenheit 9/11"

I am a soldier in the United States Army. I was in Iraq with the Fourth Infantry Division. Thank you for your movie; I know most of my fellow soldiers and I wondered day to day why were we there. "For the freedom of the Iraqi people," we were told, but day by day, Iraqi workers came into our base to work, and on those days I would ask, "Is it better that we are here?," and every time they would say worse, or the same.

Instead of worrying about just Saddam and his minions, they had to worry about everyone. I would then ask what would help, and they would state, "We need clothes, food, water, and electricity."

I was guarding some Iraqi workers one day. Their task was to fill sandbags for our base. The temperature was at least 120. I had to sit there with full gear on and monitor them. I was sitting and drinking water, and I could barely tolerate the heat, so I directed the workers to go to the shade and sit and drink water. I let them rest in the shade for about 20 minutes. Then a staff sergeant told me that they didn't need a break, and that they were to fill sandbags until the cows come home. He then told the Iraqis to go back to work.

After about 30 minutes, I let them have a break again, thus disobeying orders. If these were soldiers filling sandbags, in this amount of heat, those soldiers would be bound to a 10-minute work, 50-minute rest cycle, to prevent heat casualties. Again the staff sergeant came and sent the Iraqis back to work and told me I did not have to sit out in the sun and watch them, I could sit in the shade. I told him no, I had to be out there with them so that when I started to need water, then they would definitely need water. He told me that wasn't necessary, and that they live here, and that they are used to it.

After he left, I put the Iraqis back into the shade. I could tell by their faces that some were very dehydrated; most of them were thin enough to be on an international food aid commercial. I would not treat my fellow soldiers in this manner, so I did not treat the Iraqi workers this way either.

A few months after this, I was on the Iraqi escort detail again. We had received a bunch of housing units for the base that day, and the Iraqis finished up for the day at sunset. The problem here was that the truck drivers were contracted out from Jordan, and their trucks were low on fuel. The same staff sergeant refused to give them any of our fuel on the base, and told them they had to use the Iraqi fuel station down the highway. That was not very appealing to the drivers since the insurgents did not just attack the troops, they went after anyone who was working for us. So the drivers asked if they could stay on the base till morning, and the staff sergeant said no. So as we sat there and watched them leave the base, unarmed, unescorted, with fear and dread written on all of their faces, I could only think that if this is the way America does business with others, no wonder they want to put bombs on the side of the road for us.

This went on for 8 months while I was in Iraq, and going through it told me that we were not there for their freedom, we were not there for WMD. We had no idea what we were fighting for anymore.

## "WHERE ARE THE WMDS?
## WHY ARE WE REALLY OVER IN IRAQ?"

FROM: Jay
SENT: Friday, August 6, 2004 1:11 PM
TO: mike@michaelmoore.com
SUBJECT: Bush the almighty

I will be on active duty for at least two more years. I have been in for eight years total.

I would like to ask Mr. Bush personally why he is saying he supports us troops, yet we are still downsizing our forces and our funding continues to get thinner and thinner. They are giving people the option of getting out of certain career fields right now, closing bases on top of it. Yet Osama bin Laden is still at large; we are not even really doing anything over in Afghanistan, and the forces we do have, we are sending into a nightmare. That nightmare was a lie from the beginning.

Where are the WMDs? Why are we really over in Iraq? Why the hell are our troops dying? Mr. Bush, how are we safer now than we were before you stole office? There were a lot of people I saw when I was deployed in the desert whose spirits were down, and a lot wondered why the heck we were even in Iraq. You don't know friend from foe, and a country that DID NOT have any terrorist training camps is now thriving with them. Iraq will never be stable, another Vietnam in the making. Hope you are proud of that one, Mr. Bush, because I know I am not.

We still have people over here who are uninsured medically, homeless, jobless. Even veterans' benefits were cut. We know right where Mr. Bush's priorities lie. They are in bed with companies instead of the American people.

Mr. Bush, I have sworn to protect this country from all enemies foreign and domestic. You have gone against all American values and Americans in general in pursuit of greed and power, stepping on those who look up to you to run this country in the right direction. You have lied to all of us and sent our brave men and women off to war to die for your cause and not America's. You have also compromised the safety and security of every American in this great country, using dirty politics to scare and cheat all Americans.

The definition of a TERRORIST is: *"the systematic use of violence to create a general climate of fear in a population and thereby to bring about a particular political objective."* Sounds to me like you fit the description well, Mr. Bush.

I will do my part as a military member and American citizen to make sure to protect the country from you. That means doing my part in November, going to the polls and casting my vote, to vote you and your administration out of office. And don't think you will steal this election. There are plenty of people who are going to vote you out of office. Thanks for burning that bridge a long time ago—helps to make for an easy decision.

## "This Is All Bullshit"

From: Anonymous
Sent: Friday, July 9, 2004 9:54 AM
To: mike@michaelmoore.com
Subject: Reservist who doesn't want to go to Iraq

Mike Moore,

I am a reservist in the navy. I have been in the Reserves for 3 years and have been activated for 1¾ years (right after 9/11 for homeland security). I have recently been informed that I am to be activated again, but this time I will be going to Iraq. I am Seabee, and we will be building schools and hooking up electricity and water over there. I am not thrilled about this. Seven Seabees have already been killed trying to help the Iraqis. I have not had a chance to see your new movie, and my husband says that maybe I shouldn't. He thinks that it will make me angrier toward Mr. George W.

I just want you to know that there are many of us reservists who think that this is all bullshit. I am not looking forward to leaving my one-year-old daughter for eight months or more to fight a battle that I believe is wrong. The Iraqis don't want our help. If they did, they would not be trying to kill us.

## "THE WAR BUSINESS"

FROM: Anonymous
SENT: Thursday, July 1, 2004 6:34 PM
TO: mike@michaelmoore.com
SUBJECT: I was in the war

I wanted to personally write you and thank you. I was there in Kuwait, and remember quite vividly how despicable the whole thing was. I was a counterintelligence agent (please don't hold it against me) and an Arabic linguist. I remember people saying that we were fighting for America, or even oil, but it was apparent even at the earliest stages that this was about big business. The war business. I remember the obvious waste, and how the KBR guys would lose it if we used their phones to call home, free phones I might add. Phones that didn't have a 3-hour wait. I remember seeing entire battalions sit in a warehouse for a month, then get sent home without ever doing a thing in the war effort. I had conversations with members of these units and was told that they basically came to the war because their battalion commander wanted a deployment on his résumé.

I felt as hot as I had ever felt in the desert, and my eyes burned with tears. My heart raced, and my entire body felt as uneasy as I had ever felt during a scud alert. I relived my time in the war during that short instant in your film. Thank God I spoke my mind just enough to get sent home without getting court-martialed. After losing my sergeant stripe and some pay, I got a plane ticket home. I will make that deal any day, and I am never going back to that country in that capacity again!

I used to be a staunch supporter of the GOP. I used to toe the party line. I used to think that those in Washington cared. Now I know the truth! Democrats and Republicans are nothing more than elitists. What can be done? I can't possibly vote for the Dummy, and Kerry is no better. Same college, same fraternity, same bank account, same lying ways and half truths. These people are completely out of touch with the American people! Is there anyone in Washington who is in touch? I guess that is why I am now a registered Independent.

I haven't always agreed with you, but I will be damned if I wouldn't die protecting your right to call it the way you see it! Thank you, Michael Moore. Thank you for expressing your freedom of speech!

## "WHERE IS THE OIL GOING?"

FROM: CHRIS F.
SENT: Thursday, May 6, 2004 10:49 AM
TO: mike@michaelmoore.com
SUBJECT: A view after returning from Iraq

Dear Mr. Moore,

I was in Iraq from April 1, 2003, until March 23, 2004. I spent the beginning of the war without even the basic combat load of ammo. We were driving Iraqi city buses transporting enemy prisoners of war and trying to understand why when we stopped at a newly secured base we could not find any weapons of mass destruction. Later in the war we ended up just outside of Fallujah and stayed there until the Marines took over. There we ran another prisoner-of-war camp.

What I wanted to say is that most of my unit wants to quit the National Guard and never pick up a weapon for this current administration again. We left thinking that we were protecting the Iraqi people and the people of the United States from terrorism. When in truth we are the terrorists.

Oh, and before I forget, tell me, if U.S. soldiers are escorting over 100 trucks a day hauling oil out of Iraq, then where is the oil going?

## "What the Fuck WE Are Doing There"

FROM: Edward Dalton
SENT: Thursday, March 11, 2004 7:25 PM
TO: mike@michaelmoore.com
SUBJECT: I just returned from Iraq

Dear Mr. Moore,

I just returned from Iraq with the 101st Airborne Division after being there for eleven months.

I was the lowest common denominator in "President" Bush's foreign policy. I am just a working-class man who joined the army to pay off my student loans and all of a sudden 9/11 happens, and the next thing you know I wake up one day in Afghanistan. One year later I am in Iraq and cannot figure out what the fuck WE are doing there.

It amazes me how blind people are, especially my fellow soldiers, who suffer at the hands of Bush but still continue to vote for him. Ah, the power of the media and the fear that they instill. I am more afraid of my government than I am of the Middle East and their leaders.

Thank you for your continued efforts, your in-your-face approach, and your many years of speaking the truth. You do not have to wear a uniform to serve your country, and you have proved that time and time again.

## "PRESIDENT BUSH USED US"

FROM: O.P.
SENT: Friday, July 16, 2004 12:52 AM
TO: mike@michaelmoore.com
SUBJECT: "Fahrenheit 9/11"

I recently came back from an eight-month deployment in support of Operation Iraqi Freedom, Operation Enduring Freedom, and Joint Task Force Liberia. I returned home and am still proud to serve my country and proud to protect this nation from harm's way. Recently the commanding officer of my ship, the USS *Iwo Jima*, informed us that we will have to return for a second deployment by March 2005.

At first, I was disappointed, I wanted to know why. We just came back.

So I asked him. His response was, "The war is not over and we have a job to do in Iraq." I couldn't say anything except, "Roger that." I finally came to accept the fact that I made a commitment and I will stand by my word to defend this great country of ours. However, after seeing *Fahrenheit 9/11*, I felt as if President Bush used us.

There are no lies behind this documentary, for there is proof (literally) behind each of your words. After seeing this documentary, I will not return to Iraq for a second deployment. I will probably get arrested, discharged, or even executed according to the Uniformed Code of Military Justice.

It's about time we, the people, take a stand against President Bush. I am.

I am a United States sailor. I will support and defend the Constitution of the United States of America and I will obey the orders of those appointed over me.

I represent the fighting spirit of the navy and those who have gone before me to defend freedom and democracy around the world.

I proudly serve my country's navy combat team with honor, courage, and commitment. I am committed to excellence and the *fair* treatment of *all*.

## "WE CAN'T AFFORD THIS WAR WE ARE IN!"

FROM: SPC Matthew Burns
SENT: Thursday, July 15, 2004 5:31 PM
TO: mike@michaelmoore.com
SUBJECT: Thank you

Dear Mr. Moore,

I am a soldier currently stationed in Fairbanks, Alaska. My name is SPC Matthew Burns. I really appreciated that you didn't place the blame for our current catastrophe on the shoulders of soldiers. We carry so much already, and it is great to finally see blame where it is most deserved. I will go anywhere and do anything my country asks me to, because that's what a soldier does. I don't trust my political leaders anymore to make reasonable decisions. We can't afford this war we are in!

Our military budget is larger than that of the top ten closest in the world COMBINED, but my unit can't afford the training and equipment we need. There is always a budget problem paying for our training. I will go to Iraq if I am needed there, but it would be nice if I had the training I, and every other soldier, deserve. Where is this money going?

Regardless, I just wanted to say thanks for giving us credit for what we do. *Fahrenheit 9/11* touched my heart and that of my spouse. Give my regards to your friend in Flint who lost her son. I hope the army can give my family more than a phone call.

I am scheduled to be deployed next summer to this war I don't agree with. I will go, as I don't wish to dishonor my family or country. I know others who feel the same way. I hope our leaders can be trusted to make better decisions in the future. Oil is not worth one soldier's life lost. Too many young Americans are dying for this cause. The deaths of September 11, 2001, must not have been enough to please Mr. Bush. I hope the "thief in chief" isn't chief much longer. Thank you from the bottom of my heart.

## "I Felt Betrayed and Used"

From: Anonymous
Sent: Monday, December 22, 2003 7:21 PM
To: mike@michaelmoore.com
Subject: Could it get any worse?

Mike,

I came home from Iraq in September after nine months with the 101st Airborne Division. What I came home to was not the same country I left.

I will admit that before the war, I bought into much of what Bush was saying. Don't get me wrong, I didn't vote for him before, and I didn't trust him. Still, Saddam just HAD to have all those weapons, right? Why else would he be giving the run-around to all the inspectors? It just made sense. I didn't really believe that he posed a direct threat to us, but by God, he just HAD to have those weapons. I was never scared of being shot, or hitting a mine. What scared me to death was being on the receiving end of a chemical- or biological-tipped scud and not getting my mask on in time.

If anyone has ever seen or read about what these weapons can do, you will understand my fear. The first two days of the war we had an alert every time a missile was launched. The fear of getting that mask on as fast as you can and then waiting to see if you beat the odds or had the scud hit you is something I never want to experience again.

A funny thing happened on the way to Baghdad: we soon put away our chemical suits and gear. Saddam never launched a chemical attack. I thought that surely we had some general to thank for not following orders, since Saddam just HAD to have all those weapons. I mean Colin Powell (the one and only man in the administration whom I had any trust in) went in front of the UN and argued that point. Well, I won't bore you with the rest of the story since you know that the weapons (which Rummy claimed to know the exact location of) have never been found.

I felt betrayed and used. As an officer I am not supposed to show these feelings in front of the soldiers. We are supposed to put on a good face and ensure that the men and women we give orders to never lose sight of the mission and the task at hand. The thing was, I didn't even know what the mission was anymore. Soon other officers and I began whispering thoughts that would make Ashcroft send out the thought police. At first we skirted around it, but after a while, we began to come out and say it: We had been lied to and used.

Of course, all of you at home were being told how great our morale was and that we were happy to be doing our job. To this I said, "Of course we don't have low morale. That would imply that there is some sort of morale to measure." It was an amazing sight: thousands of soldiers not giving a rat's ass about our mission, but only wanting to stay alive long enough to get home. Does this sound like another war in our nation's past?

It makes me angry to see all this happening and knowing that people are getting away with it. I feel like a caged animal not knowing who to strike at or where to turn. I still have three years left in the army before my time is up (unless they decide to "stop loss" me and keep me in PAST the time I agreed to serve). I think the best thing I can do is to enact change from within.

I will devote my time to opening the eyes of as many of my fellow officers and soldiers as I can before the 2004 election. After all, it was probably our absentee ballots that got Bush "elected" the first time around.

If I can change the minds of enough people over the next year, then maybe we can put this whole sordid mess behind us and start fixing this great country.

(I'd give my name, but if they kick me out or send me away to Gitmo, I can't change anyone's mind.)

P.S. I think it is fair to tell you that in the mid-nineties I was a Rush-loving, Dole-voting, Clinton-bashing machine. I have now recovered from this problem and am trying to put my life back together. I hope I don't slip up and enter a tailspin like that again. My hope is that if I can change, others can, too.

## "I FEEL LIKE I HAVE BLOOD ON MY HANDS"

FROM: Dan Rackley
SENT: Friday, July 2, 2004 6:17 PM
TO: mike@michaelmoore.com
SUBJECT: Michael, I just saw your movie . . . I was moved

Michael,

Hello, my name is Daniel Rackley. I recently turned 23, and about four months ago was honorably discharged from the U.S. Navy.

I recently saw *Fahrenheit 9/11*. First thing, I have never driven two hours to go see any movie. Yours was the first. Watching your movie brought back a lot of memories of when I joined the military along with the prowar hysteria.

The first night that Baghdad was bombed, I was on watch on the USS *Bataan*. I was steering the ship while bombs were being dropped on Iraq, and some of those bombs likely came from Harriers on board my ship.

In the background while I was doing my job, a television had CNN running live coverage of the bombings. Like so many of the people who got caught up in what was going on, I started cheering and wishing death on people I didn't even know. Not just the troops, but everyone.

It didn't hit me until I saw your movie that I was driving the ship that was sending planes to kill people.

I've never killed anyone, shot a gun, or even been in any serious fights; but I feel like I have blood on my hands. I've never meant to hurt anyone, but my actions were, in part, helping to destroy houses, kill children and families. Sir, in your opinion, do you think the guilt I'm feeling is proper for me to be feeling? Or should I just say to myself that it wasn't my fault, and that I was just doing my job? My entire time in the navy, I never was put in a situation where I had to put a gun to someone's head, but in some small way, I feel like I've done it to thousands of people.

This new movie put a spark in me to get up out of my chair and get ready to make sure that things like this never happen again. I saw on your website a list of ways to take action, and I'm going to try to do as many of them as I can.

In closing, thank you for making that movie. It opened my eyes to many things. All the bullshit that people are giving you over this, tell them that Daniel Rackley says they should go to hell.

# Part II

# Letters from Our Troops Around the World

# Part II

# Letters from Our Troops Around the World

## "THE AXIS OF BUSH"

FROM: Michael Neeley
SENT: Sunday, August 1, 2004 1:47 PM
TO: mike@michaelmoore.com
SUBJECT: Taking back our country

Mr. Moore,

I want to thank you for sticking up for the common man and not bending to the media. I am stationed in Afghanistan currently and have not had the opportunity to watch your new movie, but have heard a lot about this.

I do find it appalling that our own government can spend tons of money rebuilding other countries and not rebuild our own. I also find it disturbing that we have Americans who cannot get needed medical care, but we are paying for the care of the Afghanis and the Iraqis. Thanks again for defending the rights and freedoms of those who our own government wants to forget because their CEO buddies couldn't make a buck off of it. I have to wonder what this country will be like if the axis of Bush gets another four years.

P.S. I, SFC Neeley, approve of this message!

## "PROTECTING THE RIGHTS OF OTHERS,
## YOU HAVE TO GIVE UP ALL YOUR OWN"

FROM: James
SENT: Wednesday, May 26, 2004 6:42 PM
TO: mike@michaelmoore.com
SUBJECT: Soldier writing to give thanks

Dear Mr. Moore,

I am currently 21 years of age and stationed in Bagram, Afghanistan. I have been in the military for almost three years now. I joined as a reservist, but have already spent half of my time on active duty. When I first joined back in high school, I wasn't a very good student. I spent most of my time daydreaming about what I would like to be doing. I guess I saw the military as a sort of escape. It was a challenge. It was also a lot of hype. I joined with three other friends, and we all sort of encouraged each other. I thought it would be a wonderful way to get my life on a roll. I remember when I used to talk to my recruiter, he acted like he was my best friend; he would tell me stories of all the places he had been to, all the women he'd had, and how great the military was. I guess I didn't even know what a quota was.

My whole training lasted about one year, and then I was sent home and placed on reserve status. It was the weirdest feeling going home after a year. Even though I was home, everything was just a little different. I knew I had been there before, but it almost seemed like I was living in a picture. It just didn't feel right. So many times I felt like an outcast in my own community. I just didn't feel like I fit in. I guess the military would refer to it as being better than everyone else, but I started to feel like I was just conditioned. It took me a long time to learn to relax again. After about six months of being home I really felt normal. Except I kind of grew a hate for the military.

Have you ever read the book *Siddhartha?* After years on a spiritual journey Siddhartha gives it all up and indulges in all the pleasures that he looked at as being taboo and corrupt. Like wearing nice clothes, and drinking alcohol, and gambling, and being a wealthy, greedy man. He does it for almost 20 years, then gives it all up to be a ferryman on a river. He realizes that life wasn't really making him happy, but by living it he was able to say how wrong of a life it was from his own perspective, and not just because someone had told him it was the wrong way to live.

That's kind of how I felt. Or that's how I justified what I had done. I now see the military as a kind of coldhearted cult. Telling you how to live your life. By protecting the rights of others, you have to give up all your own.

After a while I was completely happy with what I was doing. I was twenty, living in an apartment with some roommates. I was working for an ambulance company as an EMT, and I was financially independent. I was, most important, happy. That was, until earlier this year when I received a call from my unit telling me that I had been activated and had to report in two weeks.

Wow. I felt like my whole life had been turned upside down. I almost felt like I was going to break down. It was the first time I had actually cried, I mean really cried, in a long time. My parents were heartbroken and my friends didn't know what to say (they, too, hate Bush).

After two weeks or so of being activated I found out I was going to Afghanistan, and about a week after that I saw your movie for the first time. I felt like a curtain had been raised in front of my eyes. It was the first movie I had ever watched, rewound, and watched again. Words can't even describe what the movie did to me. You gave me an interest in politics; you made me realize that we aren't as free as we think. You made me really understand the propaganda that is fed to us. How arrogant we are. So much with just one little movie.

You know, we're supposed to be out here fighting for all of you, but you are the real hero, because you are fighting for us. There are a lot of people out here overseas, just like me. They don't want to be here, but they have to be. They know that they are fighting for a cause that can't be won, and that there are most likely hidden agendas. Fortunately, we have families. We have loved ones cheering us on, people we would not like to let down. After I saw your movie I so much wanted to move to Canada, and really, really thought about it, but I also thought about my family, my parents, my nieces (five and two), my nephew (two). What would they think of me? How would they remember me? As someone who was scared and ran away.

So I will wait it out. I will play the military game. I will do what I'm told, and salute when I see an officer. At least I know the truth. I know this war is a charade, but I will do my time, I will come home, and I will make sure I can spread what I know. I can do this because I know there are people like you fighting for me. Giving me hope. Again you are my hero. Please keep doing what you are doing. Even if Bush wins the election and the war continues, at least you have changed lives. At least you have awoken citizens of our country up from the slumber that is put on us.

## "Obvious Ulterior Motives"

From: Brett Sholtis
Sent: Saturday, December 27, 2003 12:26 PM
To: mike@michaelmoore.com
Subject: Letter from a guardsman in Kosovo

I'm a National Guardsman serving in Kosovo. I am writing to let you know how disappointed I am with the Bush administration and its cynical use of American soldiers for an unfounded war, a war which still has failed to achieve its questionable purpose but has cost hundreds of American lives.

Thank you for compiling the messages you've received from troops in Iraq. As a young enlisted soldier, it is vital to receive feedback other than what is carefully selected for us by *Stars & Stripes* and the nonmilitary mainstream media.

I've been deployed long enough to realize that the idealism of army values, inscribed into the minds of every basic training graduate, are values which are not upheld by many leaders, even on the highest levels of command. I've even become inured to this, realizing that we are exploited to serve the purposes of those in power.

But this war and occupation has come to disrespect all those who were trained to believe in self-sacrifice for the greater good, with no provocation, with no evidence of its supposed purposes (finding weapons of mass destruction, ending terrorism), and with such obvious ulterior motives (money, oil, a family vendetta). It seems the only way it could be justified is through an exhaustive campaign of deception and diversion. Of course, that's exactly what we've been given by the major news stations and publications.

This is very daunting to me. When *Time* magazine is awarding "the anonymous American soldier" the person of the year and

MSNBC is touting the capture of Saddam Hussein as an important victory (is it a victory to capture a man who is not guilty of possessing what we claimed he possessed?), it is daunting. When we're continuously being reminded that Saddam tortured his own people, and our soldiers are being killed by people who simply perceive themselves as defending their homeland from an invading foreign power, it is daunting. I'm only in my twenties, but it sounds like Vietnam to me.

If there is anything that could prevent this from becoming another Vietnam, it is the media, which is how I stumbled across your email: the free flow of traffic from one concerned individual to another.

I encourage you to make people see the bold distinction between the soldiers, the army, and the commander in chief. It's difficult, since the army, as any institution, is only as good as the people in it. But that's why President Bush must be seen for what he is: someone who has taken a meritorious institution composed of people who have signed a contract to serve their country, and has employed them for his own pursuits. He should be seen as a traitor to the ideals of honor and integrity. He should be seen as a traitor to all soldiers who trusted that their sacrifice would be worth something to their families and loved ones, rather than a death to serve the financial and political pursuits of one man.

## "IT'S HARD BEING A LIBERAL IN THE MILITARY"

FROM: Charles Davis
SENT: Monday, December 22, 2003 4:50 AM
TO: mike@michaelmoore.com
SUBJECT: A soldier's thoughts

Dear Mike,

I'm a PFC in the MP Corps stationed in South Korea, about 15 kilometers south of the DMZ. You know, it is really hard being a liberal in the military; you are basically shunned if you express any thoughts or ideas that are outside of the box.

When I read the letters on your website from all of the soldiers in Iraq, it really lifted my spirits to find that there are at least a few people in this idea-free military who still have a mind of their own. I am so used to being the rebel, the one who fights the power, tries to change things, and it is so hard to accept the fact that I can't openly do that here.

Every day I question why I joined, why I put myself in this situation. Maybe it was just a way to get out of the house, do something different? I do believe that it was the biggest mistake of my life.

Please tell anyone you meet that no matter how much you want to get out and see the world, or get away from your parents, or do the patriotic thing, DO NOT join the military. If you don't agree with what is going on with our government, if you don't agree with the war in Iraq, then DO NOT join the military as a way to accomplish these things.

Otherwise, you end up like me, feeling like an outsider, like you don't belong, hating what you are doing, and loathing what the people you work for are doing. And FEARING the people you work for.

Recently I went home on leave for a couple of weeks to my hometown of Alvin, Texas. While I was there, I went with my mom to a house party. I met a man there who really made me question what I must have been smoking when I joined the army. He told me about his son, who was in the first Gulf War, and how the whole right side of his body is completely paralyzed. He explained that at first they had thought it had been caused by something he had been exposed to while in Iraq, but he later learned that it was caused by the completely untested vaccine that the army doctors had given him before he went over there.

I also learned from this man (who was a professor of medical ethics and philosophy at a major university for over 20 years) that nearly two-thirds of his son's unit had debilitating results from this injection that the military gave them. Needless to say, this has scared the shit out of me. But, I thought, this was ten years ago; I'm sure things don't work like that anymore. Then this man told me of two army doctors he had just learned were thrown in jail for refusing to administer vaccines that were completely untested on humans to the soldiers in THIS Gulf War!

Jesus, I don't know what to think anymore. I don't even know if this letter makes any sense. I just want to say thank you, Michael, for everything you do. And I would like to say to everyone out there in the military who feels like I do: You are not alone. We just have to seek each other out. And to those of you who have not joined up yet . . . DON'T.

## "I Won't Say I Was Brainwashed"

From: Jacob A. Brooks
Sent: Monday, May 17, 2004 3:25 AM
To: mike@michaelmoore.com
Subject: My very changed opinion

Dear Mr. Moore,

I'm 19 years old and a member of the United States Air Force. For the last 4 years, I've been a devout President Bush supporter. Since I supported him, I did not like you very much. In all honesty, I didn't really know who you were or anything about you until I saw you at the 2003 Academy Awards. When you made your speech, I was outraged and wanted you to be thrown in shackles and locked away for eternity. . . .

Still here. . . ?

OK, thank you for not deleting this as soon as you read the "thrown in shackles and locked away for eternity" line. I assure you this is not hate mail.

I went to tech school during the beginning parts of the war in Iraq. While there, I was involved in such activities as protesting anything French related and screaming "Bush . . . Bush . . . Bush" at the top of my lungs. Most of this was led by our instructors. They'd gather us all together and give us those famous "F this and F that" speeches. They'd lead us in making fun of the French by calling them cowards and other nonsense. Throughout it all, we kept on hanging from President Bush's left nut. I WANT TO DELETE THIS, BUT IT MADE ME LAUGH TOO LOUD. Basically saying how we weren't going to be pushed around. Four months I lived in this atmosphere. Now is it any wonder why I detested you and anything else that went against President Bush?

While I won't say I was brainwashed, I definitely didn't have an unbiased point of view. I couldn't for the life of me understand why anyone would not support the war. I couldn't fathom anything bad about what this president was doing. Liberating a country! Taking down an evil dictator! Helping the world! This is what you pray every president will do.

Then I started noticing things. Eventually I was out of Mississippi and Texas and was actually out working on my own. The crazed chants and near rioting had stopped. Now, I'm stationed in a hole-in-the-wall country known as South Korea. (My military time hasn't been sweet.)

All I've been hearing about is how this many people died today and how this many died yesterday. How the people in Iraq don't even want us there. That Bush has been withholding all these files and evidence and not telling the truth about why we attacked Iraq in the first place. I'm hearing a smorgasbord of more bullshit that I don't understand at all.

Now, this is where you come in. Like I said, I haven't exactly been your biggest fan since learning of your existence. After the Oscars, I wouldn't watch your movies or even look at a copy of your book. That's how convinced I was that Bush was this holy deity handed down to us by the Good Lord himself. I mean, I honestly would get upset when people talked about *Bowling for Columbine* or *Stupid White Men*.

While at the end of my ropes, I went home to Indiana for some much needed days of leave. Confused and needing some new direction in my political life, I stumbled onto a copy of your book *Dude, Where's My Country?* I decided to push all the bullshit aside and pick it up and read it.

The things in this book blew my previously right-winged mind right off its shoulders. It seems like all the things I've been thinking about or questioning, like "Why is no one else talking about this?" It's all here. I couldn't fathom why Bush isn't in jail and/or in a shit storm from the media and concerned Americans. I mean, does no one else know all these things about him? Are you, I, and everyone else who reads your book the only people who have been educated as to these abominations? How is this man still in office?

At this point I'm probably getting carried away, but the point is that, under the circumstances, there was no way for me (along with thousands of other young airmen) to have a clear view of what's really going on in the world. I was basically driven to one very narrow-minded view.

So in closing, I guess I'd just like to thank you for your book and for having the balls to speak out against this man we actually elected to lead us. I also know you're going to get a lot of grief from America for this book and for *Fahrenheit 9/11*, which I can't wait to see, but I hope you can withstand all the negatives and keep standing up for the truth. Thank you so much for your time.

## "My Family Is Military as Far Back as I Can Remember"

From: Allison Duncan
Sent: Wednesday, July 21, 2004 3:26 AM
To: mike@michaelmoore.com
Subject: My story of the war

Dear Michael,

I was raised a staunch conservative. I lived in Pennsylvania, and my parents were Republicans. Add to that my father was a pastor and my mother homeschooled me. My family is military as far back as I can remember the stories, and I was always reading things by the Founding Fathers and writings by other great Americans. I was taught to think of liberals as emotionally driven socialist/communist-sympathizing thieves, devoid of morals who usually wanted to drive America further into a morass of ungodliness and corruption.

With this as my background, I joined the United States Air Force in December of 2001. I had signed up under the delayed entry program prior to 9/11 but did not leave for boot camp until December. I remember the indignation I felt when I watched my country being attacked. I couldn't wait to go to boot camp, and others I met on the way to Lackland AFB, Texas, felt the same way.

Fast-forward a year. I was married to a Marine from California. He was from a liberal family and voted for Ralph Nader because he hated Al Gore and thought Bush was worse. So there I was, married to someone with whom politics became a fight to the death. Oh, did I mention that I didn't talk to him for almost a week when he brought home *Dude, Where's My Country?* I couldn't believe he listened to you. And so followed my normal rampage of how awful you were and why nothing you said could be believed. Thank you, Rush Limbaugh, for that opinion. Anyway, at age 19 I, a die-hard conservative (proud member of the Religious Right), was deeply ensconced in a bed of liberalism.

After my marriage, I was stationed in South Korea for the better part of 2002 into 2003, while my husband was stationed in England. This forced me to determine things for myself for the first time. I had no one to rely on to support my positions. While in Korea, I watched the protests of hate for America outside the base. Many Koreans were angry at us for being there. It made me sick to realize that the world hated me and the country I loved so passionately. I had always thought the United States was respected and loved throughout the world. After all, as my parents pointed out, didn't the rest of the world immigrate to the States? Not many people leave the States for other parts of the world.

So then, disillusioned and no longer a bright-eyed, bushytailed member of the Greatest Airpower in the World, I finally was stationed with my husband in England.

So there I was, now with a daughter and a Marine husband who faced (and still faces) the likelihood of being sent to Iraq. Mike, I was hopelessly disillusioned with the administration. But this time, when William, my husband, asked me to watch your movies and the copies of your TV show, I was willing. I wanted to see for myself what you said. I don't agree with every opinion and statement, but I found myself nodding and becoming indignant at the injustices and hypocrisy you so easily made apparent.

Now, you know that I am no easy convert, but I must tell you the wrath you raised in my conservative Republican heart with *Fahrenheit 9/11* is burning very high. And contrary to what I would previously have thought, it is NOT burning against you. No, I find myself angry and incensed to see that the president I thought as moral and upright is so confusingly wound up in the heart of such a knot of duplicitous behavior. And now I have friends dying and fighting in Iraq. The war I supported for so long. The cause I thought just. I also face the certainty that my husband or my brother (a Marine reservist) will at some point in time be sent to Iraq.

Please know that with the knowledge you have imparted and our military experience, neither of us will be voting for Bush this election. William wouldn't have anyway, but I no longer can. To vote for him would be to foreswear the oath I took to uphold and defend the Constitution from enemies both foreign and domestic. I find myself close to tears when I realize I voted for the man I now see as the Domestic Nemesis we now face. Please keep up the good fight.

## "I Don't Want to Be a Prop"

FROM: Captain X
SENT: Saturday, January 24, 2004 4:00 PM
TO: mike@michaelmoore.com
SUBJECT: The war

Dear Mike,

I've just finished reading some of the soldiers' letters to you, and I was deeply moved by what they had to say. Because of my rank and position I cannot be as outspoken as some of them, but please know you have my support.

Having led a platoon of soldiers, I know how young and naive many of them are. They come from all walks of life, many of them joining in order to escape an impoverished past and perhaps get skills and training to bring themselves and their families to a better place. It is amazing to see the hardest gangsta thug in the world put on a uniform and proudly salute the flag, full of pride and patriotism. The army has been very good to me, by educating me and giving me the opportunity to see the world and meet America's youth.

That is why I feel sick every time I see our leaders on the television, parading around in a flight suit, dragging out our wounded for their own political gain. They even have the gall to use them as political props during the State of the Union, when in fact the leaders are the reason that the wounded have been separated from their families and subjected to violent attacks.

We are soldiers. We train for war, but a war such as this one, made under false political pretenses, shames us all. I don't want to be a prop for someone who is giving me and my soldiers tasks that are beyond our means while claiming that the military is still the proper size. I don't want to be a poster boy for a man who is willing to show the smiling faces of those reunited with their families yet refuses to allow television cameras to film the return of caskets to Dover Air Force Base. I have a duty to uphold, and I am sworn to follow the orders of those appointed over me, but I am grateful to those who will serve as our voice and say that this is wrong, and cannot be allowed to continue.

## "I Failed"

From: B. Lawler
Sent: Friday, July 2, 2004 9:28 AM
To: mike@michaelmoore.com
Subject: 36 days left in the U.S. Air Force

I've been in the U.S. Air Force for almost eight years. This August 8th I will separate from the military and move into the civilian sector. Lots of people question why I have decided to leave when I'm about halfway to retirement. I usually have to shape my answer according to who is asking.

The truth is, when I arrive to work in the morning, my stomach rolls because of what I do. I'm ashamed of what I do. In past generations serving in the military was considered an honorable sacrifice. Many brave men and women have died for the idea of America. When I look around and see what the U.S. military is, I frown. On a larger scale I start to frown at where the country is, also. What happened to this country? In a breath we have come undone at the seams.

Anyway, I will no longer willingly be a part of the U.S. military. Sometimes you have to realize you might not be on the "right side." Every time another U.S. soldier falls in Iraq, I realize the United States is one more soul away from freedom. I don't blame President Bush for this, because no one man can carry all the blame. We all are to blame. All of us.

I've earned the right to criticize. Only an ignorant man does nothing when the world around him begins to crumble. I believe you should always leave something better than you found it. In regards to my military service and the state of the forces . . . I failed.

## "Take It Out on the Enemy"

From: T.W.
Sent: Saturday, May 8, 2004 8:14 PM
To: mike@michaelmoore.com
Subject: Army brat

Dear Michael,

I'm currently working in Military Intelligence. It often seems that outside opinions of the military, and war itself, are not welcomed.

At the moment here on Fort Huachuca, where I am training, the media is looking at the training of U.S. Army interrogators because of the abuse the Iraqi prisoners are experiencing. Just hearing about what some of the soldiers are going through over in that sandbox makes me realize that, yeah, being there for months and maybe even years without simple things (your family, ample water, and good meals) can be difficult. And the army does not teach you how to manage your anger, pain, or fear. They only teach you to take it out on the enemy.

I joined right after the war started. A recruiter called me and told me about the benefits the army had to offer. Later, battle buddies and I would joke that we get paid in benefits. During my initiation ceremony, throughout basic training and especially here, while I'm finishing up my AIT [Advanced Individual Training], I'm constantly reminded that soldiers are dying in Iraq. People I trained with are there now, and I can't be selfish to think that someone else is going to fight the war for me. Thank you for taking your time to read my letter.

## "I'M POOR"

FROM: Stuart
SENT: Friday, July 2, 2004 9:48 PM
TO: mike@michaelmoore.com
SUBJECT: Gratuitous fan letter

Dear Mr. Moore,

I wanted to thank you for your eye-opening film. You don't know me from Adam, so I'll keep it brief.

I'm a damn fool currently about to start my service in the U.S. Army for the exact reasons that you put out in *Fahrenheit 9/11*. I'm poor. I need to support my family. I'm well aware that my sacrifice will mean little to the nation as a whole, but it means housing, food, and health care for my wife and child. Unfortunately, an AA, which is all I achieved, means little in our "growth" economy, save a bump in rank in the military.

After seeing your film, I despair slightly at the hell I will be most likely putting myself through to ensure my family's safety. However, I have hope that perhaps your film will make enough of an impact that I may be able to spend my time of service in peace rather than war.

## "EMBARRASSED"

FROM: Anonymous
SENT: Thursday, July 1, 2004 1:03 PM
TO: mike@michaelmoore.com
SUBJECT: Thank you!

WOW! I saw your movie last night and was floored! I'm also in the military, and I used to feel proud when I wore my uniform. I go back to work next week, and I don't think I'm going to have that feeling. Not because I don't love my country or my fellow Americans. I do, very much . . . but I feel embarrassed of what my "boss" has done and is doing. I had to take this moment to thank you.

## "DON'T DRINK AND DRIVE"

FROM: W. K.
SENT: Sunday, December 28, 2003 7:35 PM
TO: mike@michaelmoore.com
SUBJECT: SOLDIER LETTERS

SECDEF Holiday Safety Message

The following is a message sent out by Secretary of Defense Rumsfeld to all military installations. Although he addresses holiday driving safety, everyone at _____ should also be taking extra care while driving throughout the winter months. Even though the _____ community has not received much snow yet, there have been a large number of vehicle accidents involving people not following the basics of safety. Many accidents have been caused by inattentive driving, going too fast for weather conditions, tailgating, etc. It is up to everyone to practice safe driving during the winter months. As mentioned below, the consequences of ignoring driving safety can be dire.

Secretary of Defense Rumsfeld Sends

Traffic crashes are the leading cause of accidental death to our men and women in uniform. Last year, we lost 284 service members in private motor vehicle crashes. We can prevent this needless loss of lives.

During this holiday season, I am counting on each and every one of you to exercise good judgment in your celebrations. Drive defensively; wear your seat belts; wear your motorcycle protective gear. Most importantly, don't drink and drive. Have a happy and SAFE holiday.

Mr. Moore,

It's nice to know that Secretary of Defense Rumsfeld is concerned about private motor vehicle accidents:

"Last year, we lost 284 service members in private motor vehicle crashes. We can prevent this needless loss of lives."

Yes, most driving accidents are preventable, but so were the majority of the hundreds of deaths that have happened in Iraq since the "end" of the war, right? Please do not post my name/email address/base location—my wife (11 years in USAF) and I (8 years) get enough grief being the "commie pinko liberals."

## "I LOVE SERVING BUT
## NOT UNDER THESE CONDITIONS"

FROM: Dan Knight
SENT: Saturday, July 24, 2004 4:25 AM
TO: mike@michaelmoore.com
SUBJECT: My view

I have always viewed myself as a Republican and a supporter of the military. I put off seeing your movie for the wrong reasons. Since I am active duty in the USAF, I felt seeing this movie would change my view on what I truly believe is worth fighting for: freedom and how the United States helps to ensure it. I was led to believe that conditions would improve, and the cause was really worth fighting for.

I was wrong. After seeing your movie I became confused and frustrated about my role in the military. I love serving but not under these conditions. I wish the cause and the justifications for war were more real and worth fighting for, rather than being expendable. Thank you for changing so many lives. You've touched mine.

## "Drinking Was a Major Problem, as Was Drugs"

From: Tyler Scott
Sent: Wednesday, July 28, 2004 8:32 PM
To: mike@michaelmoore.com
Subject: A half-veteran

I come from a small town in Southern California, and right after high school I joined the U.S. Army for a chance to travel in Europe. After basic training (which was filled with a lot of "What was I thinking?" moments) and after a month at home, I was an 18-year-old living in Germany.

I was communications, so naturally I was stationed with others like me. And within my first week there, the last image of the all-American soldier was erased from my mind. Many of the people there were young people who were running from something else back in "real" life, and middle-aged people whom I perceived as scared to do anything else but live for the army, due to the fact that they had never done anything else. Drinking was a major problem, as was drugs. It reminded me of a high school where the bell never rang and we could go home.

Within the first months I was there, we prepared to deploy to Turkey in support of military action that might have to be done. Within six months I went from a high school student to a soldier going to war. Something did not seem right to me about what was going on, but of course I could not speak my mind openly to anyone but my family and closest friends. As the weeks went on (every week we were told was our last), it started to look dimmer and dimmer that we were deploying. And when Turkey rejected the Aid-for-Soldiers plan, the war started before we could get our equipment ready.

So we never went to Iraq, after I had mentally prepared myself for it all. So they stuck me on guard duty for six months. During all this time, I began to gain weight, and quickly. I wanted out of the army, the army that I felt had deceived me in every way once I stepped off the bus at Fort Knox. The best way to get out early and make a clean break (other than a dishonorable discharge) is to be kicked out for being overweight.

After months of yelling, arguing, and an endless stream of paperwork, I got out just in time to see most of my friends march off to war in Iraq. And every day I hope for their safe return. Many of them are still there. I took one who came home on leave to see *Fahrenheit 9/11*. It has made me a 20-year-old who will not be voting for one of the two men who caused all of this in the first place.

## "OLD GEORGIE BOY"

FROM: Mark
SENT: Tuesday, July 20, 2003 3:11 PM
TO: mike@michaelmoore.com
SUBJECT: Our new war

I am an SFC who was a weapons SGT (18b) in the Special Forces of the U.S. Army. I am no longer in the military as I was injured badly enough in a conflict in Afghanistan that I was given medical retirement.

I, and a hundred or so other chosen ones, parachuted from very high altitudes into Afghanistan only days after 9/11. They [the Taliban] hit us, so we hit them; it was only fair to me.

What began to bother me about the conflict started when "our George" began denying us the divisional support that was requested. This simply means that we were asking for very large numbers of troops so that we could cordon off the areas needing to be closed, so that we could assure the capture or killing of higher-ranking Taliban leaders, i.e., Osama bin Laden.

I strongly believe that the United States could have captured or killed Osama in a month's time had this support been given. And I only now understand why the Oval Office did not approve a full-scale attack against those that forced our citizens to either jump from a burning collapsing building, or be crushed and suffocated inside it. It was because old Georgie Boy wanted to attack Iraq, and he was saving the military divisions to complete that task. It would have been highly convenient for the president had Iraq been responsible for the attack on our soil, but they were not, and he hit them anyway. The only thing is, he didn't hit them. Instead of grabbing an old war flag out of storage and taking to the front lines to lead his men (I'm quite sure that the commander in chief could do that if he chose to) in this most important war, he stayed at home and sent a bunch of sons and daughters of the working class. Some of them even had the audacity to get killed or maimed, those damn poor people.

So George Bush has successfully avoided serving in two wars now, and I suppose that is some sort of accomplishment where he comes from. Anyway, instead of using half the troop strength and probably an 18th of the money spent in Iraq to capture or kill Osama, well, you know the rest.

I voted for Bush the first time, but unlike him, I learn from my mistakes. I think I'll give my vote to the socialists. When you're a natural-born citizen of the United States and you're jealous of Canada or France, well, you know something's wrong.

## "I Don't Even Know Why
## I Am Where I Am Today"

FROM: Jonathan
SENT: Sunday, July 18, 2004 12:19 PM
TO: mike@michaelmoore.com
SUBJECT: I'm just a Marine . . .

Dear Mr. Moore,

I'm PVT Jonathan of the United States Marine Corps. I just turned 19 and graduated high school. I went to boot camp on March 22, 2004, and in a few short weeks I'll be officially discharged from the Marine Corps for "Reactive Airway Disease" AKA asthma.

I don't even know why I am where I am today. As I sit in this computer chair in a trailer on base at Camp Pendleton, California, I wonder why I ever joined the Corps. I don't have a reason other than I thought I wanted to be a Marine. Yeah! It'd be cool to call myself a Marine. If I could go back to that day where I stood in front of my recruiter, I would have turned away and walked out that door and never signed anything.

A good friend of mine who was a loyal follower of yours always tried to convince me that I was making a big mistake and throwing my life away. How right he was. I didn't want to admit that my recruiter was a liar and that I was so gullible to sign my life away for six years. Once inside the military I realized that they don't care about you. Your purpose is to collect bullets and fill a body bag. And for what? Well, no one really knows for what right now.

Until I'm officially discharged I can't say what I would like to about Honorable President Bush. So I'll just say that I don't appreciate the lives of our armed forces being put at risk unless absolutely necessary, and somehow I think you'll agree that this "war" is not necessary. Somehow I lucked out though. I'm a Marine, and now I'm going home to my loving family and friends, and I won't have to serve 6 years. Good luck in all that you do and take care.

## "THE DEMONS THAT HAUNT ME"

FROM: Jasuan Neff
SENT: Wednesday, July 7, 2004 2:40 AM
TO: mike@michaelmoore.com
SUBJECT: Thank you

My name is Sergeant Jasuan Joseph Neff of the United States Army. I will be officially (honorably) discharged in 45 days, unless of course I am recalled (I am in the same Inactive Reserves that's been in the news lately) and I have to spend some time in jail for refusing to go.

I just finished watching your latest movie with my fiancée, and I have to say, you've captured beautifully the demons that haunt me. I was a poor kid, too. The military was my avenue away from struggle, and now the decision I made to join keeps me awake at night. When I enlisted at 17, I took an oath to uphold and defend the Constitution of the United States, against all enemies, both foreign and domestic. I mumbled the words. I may not have even said them out loud. After my indoctrination, however, that oath—the same one I may or may not have actually taken—came to mean a great deal to me.

But the contract between those who decide and those who die is bankrupt when we are betrayed the way we have been; I am honor bound to a dishonorable course of circumstance, but my greater responsibility is to the greater good. I applaud you and the troops who spoke out on film, particularly the Marine Corps corporal. Thank you for speaking for me.

## "It Sickens Me"

From: RLC2
Sent: Sunday, May 23, 2004 7:41 AM
To: mike@michaelmoore.com
Subject: Random rumblings

In a time when thousands of men and women across the services are being sent off to fight in a "war" started for all the wrong reasons by a president who did not receive the popular vote, I have to wonder, How is he able to do this? How is he just able to continue on? It sickens me. No other words can say it.

I enlisted initially and on two subsequent occasions reenlisted to defend against all enemies foreign and domestic. To me that means someone who poses a threat to me or my way of life. Neither has occurred. Do I agree with everything Saddam has done? Do I agree with anything Saddam has done? Not really. Then again, I don't really care about what my neighbor is doing, so long as he keeps it to himself. Harsh? Maybe. In any other business-type contracts I've dealt with, if conditions change greatly from the original contract, said contract is void. So why not reverse thousands of enlistments for men and women? We didn't sign on for this type of service.

If I had just a shred of evidence of a WMD or any sign that Saddam and crew had a single thing directly to do with September 11th, then things would be different. I know, I know, a lot of Iraqis don't like us. Well, no fooling. A lot of Russians, Chinese, Mexicans, Canadians, Americans, and all kinds of other "ans" and "ese" don't like us.

Hopefully the tide will turn soon, as I am witnessing a decline in the manufactured patriotism every day. The flags are being waved less, yellow ribbons have turned to yellow tattered strings from weathering, and you see fewer and fewer cars with those cute flag magnets.

I used to be able to go anywhere in my uniform and people would jump at the chance to help me—no more lines at the post office, no more paying full price for that meal. Sure those perks were nice, but you know what, it's a shame it took all this to happen. Now with the decline it shows that either we as Americans have either just accepted this as our way of life, we've forgotten what happened two and a half years ago, or your average American just doesn't care anymore.

Can you blame them? One day the terror alert is orange, the next red. Maybe we can vote on the next color . . . just like M&M's. The average American doesn't know what to think anymore; they don't need to think anymore. They have government for that! Anyone who dares challenge that has their very own patriotism challenged.

In closing I want to share with you a small bit about the life of a Vietnam veteran I met. He told me a tale of how in a time not too long ago, at this very base, people were scared to go off base. Cursed at, spit at, and just generally mistreated. Yet in this new millennium I've had people stop and want to shake my hand, give me a hug, or just say thanks. My, how times change.

I don't want to sound ungrateful but I just wonder . . . before September 11th, where was everyone at? When the smoke clears, will they still be there? What will my son's textbooks say about all this? Will people still say the military gets paid too much (even though I have brothers and sisters in arms who qualify and receive welfare)? I wonder a lot lately.

## "Blindly Following Their Leaders"

From: Robert Egolf
Sent: Saturday, July 31, 2004 10:55 AM
To: mike@michaelmoore.com
Subject: My story

A couple of years ago, in 2002, I was a soldier. I went through basic training at Fort Sill, Oklahoma. I went through my MOS [Military Occupational Specialty] training to become a 96R at Fort Huachuca, Arizona. 96R is the only all-male MOS in Military Intelligence.

Then I started listening to people protesting against the United States going to war in Iraq. I had a moral problem with going and killing someone who never did anything to me.

When I got to Jump School at Fort Benning I decided to pull out of the school. I had no permanent duty station at the time so they put me in the 1/507th Headquarters Company. I went AWOL a few days later. I finally turned myself in at Fort Knox in the last few days of October of 2002. I found out that I was dropped from the rolls a couple weeks before I got there. They classified me a deserter. Thankfully, because I was still under TRADOC, the training and doctrine command, the only thing they did was give me an other than honorable discharge under Chapter 10 of AR 635-200.

To this day I do not regret deserting the army. Soldiers follow orders and never question them when their life is on the line. They need to start asking for a good reason to put their life on the line instead of blindly following their leaders.

## "At One Point I Lost Hope in America"

From: T.C.
Sent: Thursday, March 4, 2004 1:38 PM
To: mike@michaelmoore.com
Subject: My thoughts

Hey Mike,

I just finished reading the "Letters from Soldiers" section of your website. I'm active duty military, so a lot of those letters hit close to home. The last four years of my life have been the worst, but I'm told that by serving my country, I'm doing the best thing an American can do.

For every "whopper" served to the American civilian, a whole menu of "whoppers" is prepared for the American soldier. Having recently spent time overseas in support of Operation Enduring Freedom, I've heard them all and sampled the best that the Pentagon can cook up.

I grew up in an ardently patriotic family. My family is proud to say that a relative has served honorably in every major war since the Civil War. I was brought up believing in a country that offered invaluable freedoms and opportunities, freedoms that brought my forefathers to America. Imagine my surprise when I grew up and realized that my parents' and war hero grandparents' romantic views were, at the least, outdated. Being in the military, seeing everything firsthand—imagine my dismay.

At one point I lost hope in America. I gave up on Americans, and I stopped caring. I figured all was lost, that the things that were once beautiful about our country were gone, thanks to terrible leadership (both Democrats and Republicans are guilty) and a stupid and fat society too dumb to notice or care.

A while back I watched *Bowling for Columbine*, which led me to read your books, which has led me to write this letter. Mike, I don't always agree with you, and sometimes my WASP, Republican Youth roots kick in and I temporarily hate you. But through it all I see you as one of the greatest patriots America has, one of the loudest voices of reason there is. That sounds pretty clichéd, I know, but I'm serious.

Too many Americans are lining up to receive their lethal injection of MTV, SUVs, and KFC. (You like that? That one was all mine, feel free to quote me.) You are giving a lot of these people a wake-up call. Even the people who think you are an obnoxious jerk—you've got them talking about the issues and forming their own opinions. People are thinking! People are asking questions! No wonder D.C. is squirming. I try to turn as many people on to your books as possible. If you ask me, even if people hate your books, you've still scored a victory. You've restored my faith in the American people and in our society.

Also, I'm sort of in trouble for a poster I have hanging on a wall in my military housing dorm room. It's a concert poster for the band Queens of the Stone Age. I bought it last year and had it framed. It is a cartoon depiction of G. W. Bush and says "Enjoy the music while you can" in large letters. My patriotism has come into question.

## "Proud to Be a Soldier"

From: Ben Barlow
Sent: Sunday, July 25, 2004 8:20 PM
To: mike@michaelmoore.com
Subject: Thank you

Mr. Moore,

My name is SSG Ben Barlow and I have just recently seen *Bowling for Columbine* and *Fahrenheit 9/11*. I would like to say thank you. I went into *Fahrenheit 9/11* very reluctantly, but I had to see what all the hype was about. Being in the USAF you can probably guess why. I believed everything my boss (the president) did was right, but after your movie it has really opened my eyes. Your movie did an excellent job of portraying the American soldier.

I am usually not brought to tears by a movie, but at this one I was. I hope the American people can look at us the way you portrayed us. Your movie did two things to me. It made me proud to be a soldier, and it made me really think about my affiliation with the Republican Party. Thank you again, sir.

P.S. Below is a copy of the email I sent to the President of the United States telling him how I feel.

Sir, my name is SSG Benjamin Barlow, and I am in the United States Air Force. I just saw *Fahrenheit 9/11*, and I understand this is the opinion of one man, but that movie is very damaging to your office. I voted for you in the last election, and I will support any decision you make while you're in office because that's the oath I took. Please give me a reason to support my boss while my fellow brothers and sisters in arms are dying in a war that seems to be for nothing more than financial gain and power.

## "BUSH LOVER"

FROM: A.C.
SENT: Monday, July 26, 2004 6:30 PM
TO: mike@michaelmoore.com
SUBJECT: You are brilliant!

My name is A.C. and I am a 19-year-old soldier in the U.S. Army. Seeing *Fahrenheit 9/11* was the most educational experience I have ever had in a theater. After seeing it, I was able to convince a number of conservative friends and family members to see it. Even my cousins who live in an upper-middle-class Texas town went to see it after my recommendations.

One thing in particular that I loved about your film is that you showed that the military does not get to choose its policy. Already, I have been attacked as a "Bush lover." By associating me with Bush just because I am in the military aggravates me more than anything. My service oath said I have to obey the president. It didn't say anything about liking him. I plan to vote Democrat in the next election, and I convinced most of my family to do so also.

## "He Doesn't Know What We Went Through"

FROM: Harry H.
SENT: Wednesday, July 21, 2004 4:57 PM
TO: mike@michaelmoore.com
SUBJECT: Bush

I am a soldier, and I fought with my friends in Afghanistan. When Bush was elected in 2000, I was 17, and I thought he would be the best for America, as he was a Republican. By now, I am disillusioned with Republicans in general. To hear the president speak about "liberation" is to declare to his soldiers that he doesn't know what we went through, and are still going through.

The war is not over, and is not likely to end soon—as long as we have this president in office. When I cast my vote for anyone but Bush come November, I will think of my fallen friends.

# Part III

# Letters from Veterans

(of past wars)

## "THERE IS NO EXCUSE FOR THIS WAR"

FROM: Anonymous
SENT: Tuesday, July 13, 2004 8:48 PM
TO: mike@michaelmoore.com
SUBJECT: Training soldiers

I am writing this letter as an irate veteran who spent twenty-five years as an infantry drill instructor in the United States Army Reserve. I take it very personally that many of the thousands of soldiers who I trained for combat have been sent into the hell of a war zone with little thought given to what that means. I have no way of knowing how many of those fine soldiers have mental problems, missing limbs, lost vision, other serious medical problems, or have lost their lives. We know that the number killed is now near 900, the number wounded near 7,000 to date, and one in five have mental problems because of their tours. The odds are, some of those are my soldiers.

I spent those years serving my country by trying to instill honesty and integrity in my soldiers, as well as teaching them the many skills of armed combat. I was also their counselor, their teacher, their mother, and their father. For this president to have the gall to send those soldiers into combat simply because he and his comrades wanted to do so is obscene.

The lie that he repeats daily is that Saddam Hussein would not allow the weapons inspectors to do their job. Bullshit! There were over 400 UN inspectors in Iraq going anywhere they wanted to go including the presidential palaces, when Bush pulled the plug and invaded a sovereign nation, breaking international law in the process.

I pray that the number of Americans going to see *Fahrenheit 9/11* quadruples by the time of the election. Thank God, somebody has stood up for our soldiers and their families left suffering here at home. This phony war represents the biggest military mistake ever made in the history of this country, and my soldiers are dying because of it. That is not to mention the untold thousands of innocent Iraqi civilians killed by the weapons of war.

There is no excuse for this war. There is no excuse for this president or his minions.

Those outstanding individuals who serve this country do not deserve to be thrown into the path of roadside bombs, rocket-propelled grenades, machine-gun fire, and small-arms fire based on lies. Trust me, these weapons kill just as easily as a weapon of mass destruction. Yet this president sent our soldiers into combat thinking they would face weapons of mass destruction. What kind of person would do that without exhausting every possible alternative and taking all of the time in the world instead of rushing headlong into a war with no end? Now you know why I am furious!

## "PEOPLE NEED TO KNOW"

FROM: Sally Drumm
SENT: Tuesday, July 6, 2004 9:15 PM
TO: mike@michaelmoore.com
SUBJECT: Thank you

Dear Mike,

I spent 20 years of my life in the Marine Corps. You nailed it when you said the volunteer force would do their jobs and do them well as long as they are not sent into harm's way unnecessarily. I had wondered if any of the troops in Iraq know what they are fighting for. After seeing your film, I know they will know the truth. Thank you. I am glad the people seeing your film will have to face their defense by the poorest of the poor, who are kept that way so the ranks can be filled generation after generation.

I appreciate you showing the footage of Iraqi citizens suffering and dying because this is the reality of war that has been missing from American media coverage. People need to know.

Thank you for reaching without fear or hesitation into the American soul. You have told the truth that so badly needed to be told about the dysfunctional Bush administration.

You have done justice, and your doing it makes me feel good about being part of this country for the first time since the 2000 election. I hope you never give up or give in.

## "I Consider Them My Brothers"

From: Paul Mullen
Sent: Tuesday, July 6, 2004 11:39 AM
To: mike@michaelmoore.com
Subject: Painful

Mike,

I'm a former infantry officer in the U.S. Army. I finished my service on March 19th, 2001 (exactly two years before the invasion of Iraq).

I have a lot of friends over there. I would, in many cases, consider them brothers. I saw your movie and saw the footage of the soldiers. It was so real to me . . . how they spoke and acted. I felt as though I knew every one of them. After I left your movie I have never cried so hard as an adult.

Every time I turn on the news, these days, I'm haunted by the idea that I may see one of my brothers lying dead on a Baghdad sidewalk. Your movie was the most painful media viewing I have ever had to endure. Thank you for making it for us.

## "Nobody Loves Peace Like a Soldier"

From: Bob Schaefer
Sent: Friday, July 16, 2004 9:59 PM
To: mike@michaelmoore.com
Subject: I joined the army when I was 17

I joined the army when I was 17 years old, back in 1972. I did it because I was patriotic, and, well, kinda dumb.

In my time in service, it was an interesting period where the last of the draftees finally got out, and it was just us volunteer types left. And I think it was a very good thing when the all-volunteer army finally took hold. It was a careful balance of people who lacked opportunity getting the chance of a lifetime to be somebody important. On the other side of the balance was the army's commitment to take care of its people. It's worked well, now, for 32 years.

Implicit in that balance was the old Drill Sergeant's motto, "I'll never ask you to do anything that I wouldn't do myself." (Envision a powerful, muscular, black drill sergeant in front of a 140-pound weakling.) The volunteer army is based on trust. We trust the heads of the four forces to never ask us to do anything that they wouldn't do themselves, or haven't done themselves in the past. We trust them to be the wise soldiers that they are, soldiers who don't invite war. Nobody loves peace like a soldier, they say.

I am afraid that history will write that one of the biggest casualties of this Bush debacle will be the armed forces, in particular the all-volunteer army. It was a delicate thing of beauty and balance, which unfortunately has been upset by a few wild-eyed chicken hawks. I don't want to mention any names—Cheney, Rumsfeld, Wolfowitz.

But you know what? I think I still have an inherent sense of trust that, ultimately, officers of wisdom and judgment will prevail. This has to be a temporary thing. It's a two way street. The army brass knows that it has to take care of its people. Right?

However, I think we're also to the point where the brass have to stop complimenting the emperor on his new clothes. If someone in the brass would just have the conviction to stand up and say something, it would go a long way to helping restore the trust between the enlisted men and the Pentagon brass.

In the silence, soldiers in Iraq gather rocks as they go out on patrol, for the inevitable rock fights they will have with children. Meanwhile, the United States is building the largest embassy in the world in Baghdad. Who's going to step forward and say "up" is "up" and "down" is "down"?

## "I CALL MYSELF AN AMERICAN"

FROM: Ray Perkins
SENT: Saturday, July 3, 2004 2:46 PM
TO: mike@michaelmoore.com
SUBJECT: A veteran's email to the president

After seeing *Fahrenheit 9/11*, I sent an email to the White House. The White House director of communications Colby Cooper stated in an official White House email response that "Iraq was the central front on the war on terror."

Just when and why did this exactly become policy? Was it perhaps all the WMDs that Iraq had or the thousands of al Qaeda training camps supposedly in Iraq? I recall that Iraq's WMDs were President Bush's reason to the world to go to war in Iraq. I think that if Iraq really had WMDs, the invasion would have been justified because it would have been a clear and repeated violation of UN Resolutions.

I have not seen any valid or clear connection between al Qaeda and Iraq. Could it be because there was not a credible connection? Going to Iraq has hurt the war on terrorism, and the world is starting to realize that.

The leadership of this country lied to us. We have found nothing! Is it just me, or do you realize that Osama bin Laden is still walking the face of the earth? Almost three years later and you still don't have him? You shouldn't be reelected on that point alone. Makes me sick to think about it. "We the people," Independents, liberals, and right-wingers alike, want his head on a platter. The world is not, and will not, be a safer place after Iraq. We have most likely created many more Osama bin Ladens, and will be fighting them long after we have tried to forget about the Bush presidency.

Correct me if I am wrong, but I don't recall any Iraqis being on the planes that flew into the Trade Center. I do recall many of them being from Saudi Arabia. It probably wouldn't be "prudent" to look at that, would it? It would most likely hurt the Bush family business to take a hard look at the Saudis and put the screws to them. I am neither a Republican nor Democrat. Like many former veterans, I call myself an American. I prefer decisions in Washington to be made for the good of all Americans, and not for the good of one political party or another.

For four years of my life I put on a military uniform every day, like millions before me, and stood a post to protect freedom. Being an American, you are born with God given rights, but being a veteran means that you have earned them, for yourself and for others.

Mr. President, I am evoking my First Amendment right to express my displeasure of your leadership. I hope that exercising my First Amendment right is not a violation of your Patriot Act. There is nothing patriotic about it, and it is a contradiction in terms. Hopefully the Patriot Act will be repealed someday, at the expense of my tax dollars.

I did not spend four years in the army putting up with training, formations, road marches, eating MREs, freezing my ass off, heat exhaustion, living in tents, bugs, digging hundreds of fighting positions, missing my friends and family, getting shot at, learning how to kill other human beings, etc., etc. I did not spend four years in the army to watch another soldier ask for his mother while he sucked his last breath to have you take my freedoms from me or other Americans.

I have always been proud to be an American, but lately, after all you have done, I feel ashamed. You have not made America safer or the world a better place to live. Also, American credibility is forever tarnished in the eyes of the world. That will be your legacy, Mr. President, and many books will be written about it.

As President Truman once said, "The buck stops here," and "here" is at your desk, Mr. President. Come this November I think "we the people" will be asking for our change.

## "YOU CALL THIS FREEDOM?"

FROM: Z.M.
SENT: Tuesday, December 23, 2003 11:18 PM
TO: mike@michaelmoore.com
SUBJECT: Troops

Being an air force veteran I would like to add to what you have said in regards to supporting our troops. Many of our troops are being taken advantage of by a military recruiter who has lied to them in some form or another. Military recruiters prey on young, vulnerable men and women, constantly lying to these new recruits, filling their minds with false information such as, "You'll never go to war," or "You can leave whenever you want in the military; it's up to you."

These lies are told to young men and women each and every day, young men and women who are looking to remove themselves from a below-average home life, young men and women who are looking to get out of small-town America and see what the world has to offer them, young men and women eager to serve their country because they see this war glorified on TV every day.

I'm not sure who is ultimately to blame here, but what needs to be understood here is that young men and women are being taken advantage of by these glorified car salesmen with short haircuts on a daily basis, and for what? Just to put another dime in Curious George's pocket. To say that our troops are involved in this war "because they want to be" is a false statement as it obviously does not apply to all troops. You call this freedom?

## "I FELT SOLD OUT"

FROM: Lori L.
SENT: Friday, July 9, 2004 9:33 PM
TO: mike@michaelmoore.com
SUBJECT: Female Desert Storm vet thanks you!

Dear Mr. Moore,

Your movie was moving, breathtaking, and bitterly sad. My tears flowed. More importantly, I have been awoken. I plan to be MUCH MORE ACTIVE in politics now that I have been shown what the media doesn't tell us.

I spent seven months at Desert Shield/Storm; it was miserable, frightening, and a joke. An absolute joke. I, and many in my unit, thought it was a sham that we were there and that oil was the price for our lives. I felt sold out. Our servicemen and -women are dying for a lying president who would rather golf than deal with reality. A man who doesn't know an honest day's work, let alone the experiences of war or serving his own country. How dare he let thousands of soldiers die for this sham of a war.

I am sad to say such things of the leader of our dear country, but our country is not the same country for which I gave years of my life back in the Desert Storm era. We have lost international respect, dignity, and honor.

## "WE AREN'T ALWAYS IN THE RIGHT"

FROM: Bill Cordeiro
SENT: Saturday, July 3, 2004 10:45 PM
TO: mike@michaelmoore.com
SUBJECT: Thank you

Michael,

Thank you. I wanted to say that right off the bat to let you know how I feel. As a former U.S. Marine, I take a lot of pride in saying I am an AMERICAN. I've never been into politics until recently, and your movie has made me so disgusted at the way our country is being controlled. Honestly, I don't give a crap about what politicians are doing, as I believe most of them are full of BS, which is really no surprise to anybody. However, when I hear of my brothers and sisters dying in another country for which there is no purpose it straight PISSES ME OFF.

I know what it's like to be 19, in the military, and completely obedient to orders. These heroes will not challenge the tasks laid before them. They will risk everything they have because they believe blindly in their leader. A leader who in my eyes is becoming more and more "the Enemy." Never have I ever disliked a president in office. Never have I ever even cared what was going on in our government. But it doesn't take a genius to figure out something is wrong when every time you turn on the news, you hear about two or three more U.S. troops killed.

I spent two of my Christmas holidays in Kuwait. I believed in us helping Kuwait in the 90s. We had an honorable purpose for being there. If I were called to active duty today to serve in IRAQ, I'd enjoy nothing more than to tell Bush directly to KISS MY ASS!

Michael, on a personal note to you, I've never read your books. I've never seen your *Columbine* movie. Many of my friends don't like you, mostly in part because you are a liberal. I don't care if you worship frogs as a religion, but I know this: After all the negativity that people around me have portrayed about you, I applaud what you have done for me and this country. I hope your movie has an extremely huge impact on this country and opens everyone's eyes to the fact that, yes, we (our country) can be the bad guy. We aren't always in the right.

## "I LOST MANY TO VIETNAM"

FROM: Thomas Young
SENT: Thursday, July 29, 2004 5:24 PM
TO: mike@michaelmoore.com
SUBJECT: Some just don't get war . . .

Dear Michael,

In 1967–68 I was a high school kid who looked for every war protest in every city in California just so I could smoke a joint, check out the chicks, and have fun. I did not know what a big deal Vietnam was until just before I turned 18, when I began to realize that "The Dirty Little War" in Southeast Asia was about to hit home when a friend went missing and turned up on a hospital ship off the coast of Vietnam. He had gotten loaded on LSD and joined. We picked him up in San Francisco, California, and that's when we saw what the protests were all about. But was it . . .

In 1970, with a draft number of 263, there was no chance of me going off to war any time soon. But something clicked inside me. My friend who came back was a veggie, and others were dying. I had to find out what the fuss was all about.

Two years later, after two tours in Vietnam, on my way to my new military assignment in jolly old England, I was a total wreck. A drunk, a very sick man, and no longer a teenager, but a man who had aged beyond my years. Now I saw that war as something horrific and terrifying.

Looking for a joint or chick at a protest rally was no longer an option, but stopping the war was, when I was sober, but not while in the military. I had discovered a war that had taken my soul and left me empty inside. A war that took many a friend, either in a body bag or in their minds. I lost many to Vietnam.

Today I am well. It took many years of hard drinking, a couple times in prison, world travel, and more, but finally I found my soul and took control of my life once more. I was helped by my fiancée and best friend, my lover and writing partner, and today we share the anger and pain of a new war. Now I watch another time and another place, Iraq, and I shake with rage.

In 1991 I knew that George Bush I was a liar about Kuwait and Saddam's invasion of that country. Then came Bush II, and I tried to warn everyone about the lies and deceit of the son.

I sent letters to soldiers telling them about Vietnam and the difference between hell and war, that both were places that would rob you of your soul. No one listened. Bush invaded, and we are going on two years of war in Iraq.

## "WE MADE THIS COUNTRY AND WE FOUGHT FOR IT"

FROM: Ed
SENT: Sunday, December 28, 2003 12:55 PM
TO: mike@michaelmoore.com
SUBJECT: "Dude, Where's My Country?"

Hi Mike,

I'm reading your book and also your web page. I'm impressed and it's not easy to impress a 73-year-old. I've seen just about everything, and you appear to have what it takes. I am a two-tour veteran of the Korean War (whoops, I mean police action). Had a destroyer blown out from under me killing many young men like the ones you speak of in Iraq.

This whole thing over there goes beyond reason, except what you write about. Yeah, I saw your big moment on TV and you became my hero. That took real guts. We are very proud of you. I have spent 50 years trying to get the VA to live up to their contractual promises only to get shoved off into deliberate indifference and slow-walked until I wear out.

Can you imagine what these wounded and harmed young people are going to deal with when they get home—if they do? They will be ignored, shoved aside, and forgotten. If you are rich and connected, you wouldn't be in the service in the first place.

We made this country, and we fought for it. Let's take it back.

# Part IV

# Letters from Home

(from family and
friends of troops)

## "MY HEART IS HEAVY"

FROM: Robin Vaughan
SENT: Tuesday, January 20, 2004 11:30 PM
TO: mike@michaelmoore.com
SUBJECT: A mom who is weary of being afraid—my son will be leaving for Iraq

I am wondering if this is the last Christmas I will spend with my son.

My son is leaving on deployment to Iraq. My heart is heavy, and I am frightened. I can remember my infant son in my arms the day he was born, and I recall how I promised to take care of him and keep him out of harm's way; good luck was with me for twenty-two years. Naturally he had his share of stitches as well as a broken leg, but he was healthy, happy, and safe.

One day, my son enlisted in the army. His young idealist thoughts were that his service in the army would help him in the future with his education. I wasn't pleased about the enlistment, but I supported my son since this is what he wanted to do. Kevin enlisted prior to Sept 11, 2001.

My son is no longer an infant; he is an adult doing everything a young man can to be supportive of his country, and fellow troops. He serves with hope and courage, but I can see the fear in his eyes. Even though he is a mature man, I am still his mother. I cannot imagine someone torturing my son; I cannot imagine someone killing my son. My mind cannot wrap itself around such horrific thoughts, so my heart is in my throat. I cannot protect him, and regardless of how many times I review the situation, I cannot find a way to feel positive about his forthcoming deployment.

I will strive to have courage; I will not let him see my tears when he leaves as I know his mind needs to be on the task at hand.

I will, as I always have, support Kevin, love him unconditionally, encourage him, and do all I can to help keep him alive through his tour in Iraq.

I'm tired of being afraid of being labeled as someone who is less than a patriot because I do not support this war. I do support the men and women of our armed services as a daughter, wife, sister, and mother. My family has served many times over. I would rather see my son in Afghanistan, searching for the murderers who attacked the United States, than see this deployment to Iraq.

We will have Christmas together, Kevin and I and a group of other soldiers he frequently brings home for the holidays. I won't let them see how tired I am.

However, I feel like a traitor to my son. After all these years of keeping him safe, he is now in the hands of strangers who don't have his best interest in mind, strangers who have their own agenda, strangers who will never know my worry, my love, or my pain. These strangers are my own government, who see my own son as some stranger to be used to further an agenda that serves only themselves.

## "DEATH IN IRAQ HAS A FACE"

FROM: Margaret Reimer
SENT: Wednesday, April 21, 2004 9:50 PM
TO: mike@michaelmoore.com
SUBJECT: President Bush killed my student today

Dear Mr. Moore,

I thought you might like to know about the crappy day I had today.

While I was at the Maine Mall in Portland, Maine, getting my hair done and buying a purse to carry at my son's wedding next month (things that now seem incredibly petty and pointless), one of my English students from the University of Southern Maine was having the worst day of her young life.

Her husband, a 24-year-old National Guardsman from the Maine 133rd Engineering Battalion, was killed about 2 AM Maine time this morning in Mosul. Chris, the dead young man, was a former student of mine. This incredibly stupid war now has a face and a name, and I find I can't quit crying.

I was on my way home when Maine Public Radio announced the name of the soldier who died. I had to pull over onto a side road in Webbs Mill (believe me, it's all side roads out there) so that I could phone my husband and vent my grief and rage. Besides, it's not safe to drive while sobbing. I don't want it to seem that I believe that Christopher Gelineau was any more valuable than any of the other 600 soldiers who have died in Iraq to date, or more valuable than the thousands of Iraqis who are dying every day. However, I knew him, and I know his wife, Lavinia, and I cannot bear to think of the burden of grief that she now must carry.

Chris was the kind of freshman lit. student whom adjunct faculty pray to get in their classes. He was bright, motivated, willing to question. He read the works assigned and actually seemed to engage in the ideas. I teach literally hundreds of students a year, so he had to be exceptional to stand out in my mind after three years. Part of what made him memorable was that we had to adjust his end-of-semester work to fit in with an early call-up for Guard training.

It was the beginning of a long, problematic relationship with the Guard for Chris. Like many young people, he joined up thinking that he was not only able to do a service to his country (like helping out when his hometown flooded or providing assistance when Maine got slammed by another massive ice storm), but he'd also have money for his college education. Unfortunately, being in the Guard made being a student more than a little difficult.

Mine was not the only class in which he had to go to the professor to beg for an adjustment in the syllabus in order to finish. Eleven months ago he got married to Lavinia, a fellow student, here from eastern Europe, studying English and marketing. This semester, Lavinia enrolled in my Ancient Masterpieces class, stopping by early in the semester to ask permission to miss two classes so that she could complete her driver's ed class. Chris had been called up before he could finish teaching her how to drive, and she was now stuck in a town with terrible public transportation and no legal way to drive her car.

For the first couple of weeks of class (which doesn't finish till nearly 7 PM), I drove Lavinia back to her apartment, worrying that this fragile young woman would not make it back safely through the cold and the dark. She took to stopping by my office when she had a moment (with a double major and a job, she's a busy young woman). She would tell me about the latest email from Chris, or her plans for celebrating their first anniversary (with him 3000 miles away), or about the nights when she was gripped by terror and couldn't sleep—normal student concerns.

She'd email me with pictures of her kitties, or with a link to an article that mentioned Chris, or with forwarded messages about topics she thought I might be interested in. She was particularly concerned about cell phone radiation and was worried I might run a risk for brain cancer because I use my cell phone to talk to my husband. Last week she gave me a roll of slide film of her wedding, which I had volunteered to scan for her so that she could see the pictures. She told me happily about her plan to use the scanned photos as a surprise for Chris—I wasn't to hurry, she could get packages to him in about three weeks . . . I finished scanning those photos tonight.

Death in Iraq has a face—it's a sweet, young face, smiling, looking adoringly toward the beautiful bride on his arm. Chris was 24. Lavinia is too young to be a widow.

I will do anything in my power to get President Bush out of office. He did this horrible thing. He asked sacrifices of fine young people that he was never willing to ask of himself. He lied, he cheated, he hid, and he lied some more—and Chris paid the price.

I was already motivated about the fall election. I support MoveOn financially. I'm signed up for every anti-Bush website I can find. I am running for my local State House seat. I ran my local Democratic caucus. I cohosted a meet up for Congressman Tom Allen a month ago (part of his Reclaim America effort—not a fund-raiser—a consciousness raiser)—70 people from three little tiny Maine towns (all traditionally Republican, by the way) showed up.

This Sunday I'm hosting another. Chris is coming, although there's no way that he can know that. I'm going to print some of his and Lavinia's wedding photos, and I'm going to make sure that everyone who comes to my home on Sunday afternoon sees them. I am going to go after Bush in Chris's name. I owe him that much.

## "This Is Personal for Me"

From: Anonymous
Sent: Saturday, July 10, 2004 10:28 AM
To: mike@michaelmoore.com
Subject: Working with the troops; and a son serving . . .

I work 40-plus hours a week at an air force base in Washington State, at the Tricare Service Center. I deal with returning troops, and ones who are deploying. I love these people. I hear the agony of the families, and see the injuries both physical and mental our soldiers have suffered in this insanity.

My eldest son (21) is in the USAF. This is personal for me.

When I saw Lila, the woman in *Fahrenheit 9/11* whose son was killed in Iraq, weep, I wept, too. My heart is breaking to see what Bush and his administration have done to our people. I've been literally sick since my son signed on the dotted line, just weeks before 9/11. In my gut, I knew. . . .

Bush was here for a brief trip to Spokane earlier this year, and I am ashamed at the thoughts going through my head, of what I'd like to do to him, as he graced our streets here. I guess desperation does that to you.

Education is the key, here. We have to take our country back . . . thank you for being a catalyst to that!

## "HE WAS SO EXCITED TO
## GET OUT AND START HIS LIFE"

FROM: Michelle
SENT: Friday, July 8, 2004 10:05 AM
TO: mike@michaelmoore.com
SUBJECT: My soldier story

Hi Michael Moore,

My boyfriend was scheduled to get out of the Marines in early
September—that's when his four years were finally up. He was
sent to Afghanistan after 9/11, served six months in Iraq in 2003,
and in May they decided to send him back. Tomorrow, he was
scheduled to start the process of finally getting out.

Last week I got a call from his dad saying that he had been
injured, but that he only had a broken arm. We waited four days
until he was flown to Germany, and then we found out that there
was nothing wrong with his arm but he had a skull fracture and
part of his brain was bruised, and he is unconscious.

Yesterday he was flown to D.C., and they let us know about
the piece of shrapnel that went into the left side of his head and
out underneath his right eye. Now on top of possible brain dam-
age (we won't know for sure until they stop sedating him and he is
conscious) he will probably lose the sight in his right eye.

It just sucks. He's 21 and not even a fucking citizen of the
United States. He was so excited to get out and start his life and
move on from all of the crap he's been through in the last four
years, and now we don't know if he'll be able to talk, go to school,
walk, etc.

When I watched *Fahrenheit 9/11* a couple weeks ago, I was
really pissed at first when the soldiers were portrayed as these

crazy kids who think they are in a video game. While it may be somewhat true, you hit it dead-on later in the film when you said, "How can we expect these kids to handle war when those in charge are corrupt?" I really appreciated you spending so much time talking about the soldiers and letting the American public know the hidden story behind those who enter the military today.

I don't know how many arguments I have gotten in with people when they tell me that it is my boyfriend's fault because he chose to join the military and he knew what he was getting into. True, he had a choice, but when you fool around in high school and don't have the grades or discipline for college right away, and you turn 18 and are left to fend for yourself, what other choices are there?

Plus, he has said many times that he signed up to fight and protect American lives and has no problem doing that, but the war in Iraq has gone too far. He always said when he gets out he wants to be a teacher so he can let those kids like him know that school is important so they don't end up dead at 21 in the military.

Thanks for letting me vent. I'm so glad and he's so lucky to be alive, but I don't want to be in the hospital room when he finally gains consciousness. He is going to be so pissed because he was so close to getting out of the military and finally starting a new chapter in his life.

What can I do? I feel so helpless and have been against the Bush administration and the war in Iraq since day one, but now I need to turn my sadness and anger into something productive and help prevent someone else from having to go through this pain.

## "What Do You Say to the Widow of a Soldier Killed in Iraq?"

From: G.J.C.
Sent: Wednesday, May 5, 2004 7:08 AM
To: mike@michaelmoore.com
Subject: Widow of soldier killed in Iraq

Dear Michael,

What do you say to the widow of a soldier killed in Iraq? Especially when she's a student in your 9th-period class. Yesterday, a young lady came back to school. Her 19-year-old husband was killed in this ridiculous "war." Her life is upside down. Instead of preparing for the prom, graduation, and spending the summer at the Jersey Shore, she can look forward to visiting this young man's grave and trying to figure out how to move on.

What should I say to her? I think I know how my father felt when he was a teacher in 1969 and he was in the same situation. I feel guilty for allowing this unjust war. I feel guilty that the rich pay for young people to die for them. I feel that something needs to be done.

It's time to bring our soldiers home and admit that we are responsible for thousands of deaths. John Kerry understands war. He showed that by having the courage to stand up to what he considered an unjust war. Maybe he can do that now. Continue the fight.

## "Put Me to Work"

From: Dante Zappala
Sent: Friday, February 20, 2004 1:00 PM
To: mike@michaelmoore.com
Subject: A brother in the service

Dear Mike,

I've written this letter to you over and over in my head. From the time I saw your first documentary to sitting in a holding tank in a San Francisco jail a year ago, what I might say to you constantly fills my mind. I never compose it or send it because I keep thinking, Well, he's too big now, what would his concern with little old me be? Trivial and insecure, but I'm an American, so I'm entitled to such behavior.

I'm writing you now because my brother is going to Iraq next week. He's got arguably the worst job in the world—convoy-security in the Sunni Triangle. We're a peace-loving, war protesting family. My brother is a foster child who joined the army to get money for his son and be a better father than his own. And now his mission is to come back alive, and, in the process, he is being trained to run over children who stand in the way of the convoys because they could be potential threats. Kids like his own, kids who may just want to get food. He's at Fort Dix practicing, knocking over cardboard cutouts.

My question, hope, whatever it is . . . I am teaching here in L.A. I fill whatever the need is here in South Central. (Sorry! South L.A., we got a name and image change—how easy!) There's a thread running through this place, through Philadelphia where we were raised, through Wilkes-Barre where my brother's guard unit is located.

What is my charge, Mike? Like so many, I want to do so much. I fight apathy with optimism, with idealism, with anger. I fight frustration with hope. And now, it's my brother. Now it's my nephew who has lost his dad for an 18-month tour.

Put me to work. Just put me to work. My story is so common yet unheard. I want to get it out. I want to be put in your service, out here in L.A.; I think I can help. I'm one of many, I believe, beset with the compulsion to make a difference.

## SECOND LETTER

### "YESTERDAY, WE HEARD THAT HE WAS KILLED . . ."

FROM: Dante Zappala
SENT: Tuesday, April 27, 2004 11:07 AM
TO: mike@michaelmoore.com
SUBJECT: Some unfortunate news . . .

Dear Michael,

I wrote to you two months ago. I told you the story of my older brother, a foster kid who joined the army to support his own son. He was called to service in Iraq at the beginning of this year. Yesterday, we heard that he was killed in an explosion in Baghdad.

We are, undoubtedly, a strong family. My younger brother and I search for answers, our worst fears having come true. Our parents instilled in us a sense of responsibility, a sense of care, a sense of peace. We maintain that charge, even more so today.

Allow us to help you in any way we can. The real stories are not being told. You have made this clear: We are faced with the monumental task of doing the simplest thing—telling the truth. I want the truth to be heard and the image to be real as we approach such an important period of decision making.

I hope that, in this time, others can sense this feeling. I hope they begin to tire of the preschool food fights we see in politics and the media. I hope they receive more than just a sensational glimpse into reality. News bites are not reality. Political grandstanding is not reality. Reality is when your sister-in-law calls you to tell you her husband is dead. Reality is trying to explain this to his nine-year-old son.

After I first wrote, you extended to me a kind and touching response. I, therefore, wanted to pass along this sad piece of information to you. We are determined to prevent the deaths of other soldiers—the sons, fathers, and brothers still faced with the same incredible consequence that my own brother realized yesterday.

Nothing will ever replace this loss. My brother was one of a kind, a true gift to us for the 30 years we had him. May we all do what we can to honor him and the countless other human victims of this atrocious conflict.

## "ARE YOU WILLING TO SEND YOUR CHILD TO IRAQ?"

FROM: M.B.
SENT: Sunday, March 7, 2004 9:56 PM
TO: mike@michaelmoore.com
SUBJECT: My son is in Baghdad

Dear Mr. Moore,

I know you won't read this, but I will hope that you do. My stepson, Michael, was sent to Baghdad on February first. He was sent into a fraudulent war, by a fraudulent president, and by a group of thugs and criminals inhabiting the White House.

I'm in Michigan, and I watch the jobs here being outsourced daily, and the people suffer. I have watched my mother file for bankruptcy and sell her furniture for money to pay for her medication.

For three and a half years I have been marching against this administration, these frat-boy thugs who stole our White House. I have been interviewed by the *Washington Post* to speak out for the families of the soldiers and for the soldiers themselves, I have racked up a phone bill calling my congresspeople, and have done what I can with the limited resources I have.

I am reaching a point of despair and anger that I cannot express, as are many other people who see the truth, I'm sure. Today, when ten bombs exploded in Baghdad, I sat in terror, as I will sit for a year worrying horribly for my stepson as civil war erupts. As the people of Baghdad and Iraq turn to the reservists and guard troops of 18, 19, 20 years old and say, "Get out!," I think of the fatcats from Halliburton sitting in the leather chairs swilling brandy and chuckling to themselves about how much they made on their short-term profits. Meanwhile, my stepson stands in 120-degree heat and emails me:

"Hey Mom . . . send me some snacks . . . man we are really hungry . . . one of the guys detonated a roadside bomb, and a mob of about 250 people outside the prison here are protesting. But don't worry! I won't die, I'll come home someday . . . send me some Famous Amos cookies if you can . . . I love you . . . Mike."

He's 21. He's a reservist who signed up for the weekends. Wanted to be a cop someday. The only jobs here pay $5 an hour, and he figured it would help him to get some free training.

No matter how hard we tried to talk him out of it, he went. He was afraid not to.

Now, I am pleading with you for one thing. Let me help. I can write so many letters; I can fax so many congresspeople; I can be interviewed by so many newspapers. I am not afraid of anyone anymore. I am not afraid to speak out and say what I think, and I am very vocal. What have I got to lose? Our kid, that's what. It's Katy Bar the Door for me now.

I want to go down to D.C., I want to walk into every senator and representative's office who does NOT have a kid in the service and ask them if they are willing to enlist THEIR son for this fraudulent war that they refuse to take accountability for. They refuse to question Bu$h about it; they refuse to even bring it up.

I call all the Republican senators who never served and who have kids who are my stepson's age, and I ask them, "ARE YOU WILLING TO SEND YOUR CHILD AS A SOLDIER TO IRAQ?" I ask them to put their money where their mouth is—I ask them if they want me to come down there and bring them enlistment forms. They hang up on me. I don't have a camera crew; I don't have the money. I have the time, though, and I have the chutzpah.

If you can't use me to do that, then use me for something else. If I don't put this anger somewhere, this outrage, I may sink into despair. You have the connections and the camera crew. I don't. I thank you for what you are doing, but realize this also: There is nothing more dangerous to the Bu$h administration than an angry mother of a soldier in Iraq. An angry enlightened mother is a powerful tool to use.

In the meantime, here's a prayer for a kid in Iraq, if you don't mind. A teenager with a gun who is scared and doesn't want to be there. His name is Michael. He's from Michigan.

## SECOND LETTER

### "I GUESS I HAVE TO BELIEVE IN A GOD . . ."

FROM: M.B.
SENT: Monday, August 8, 2004 5:04 PM
TO: mike@michaelmoore.com
SUBJECT: RE: FW: Your letter to Michael Moore

Since I last wrote to you, my husband and I have been involved in antiwar activities, even with the limited resources we have in a small town. From standing on our street corner with signs, to being interviewed by *Le Monde* and any number of radio interviews. I have been working my butt off from February to June, when my husband had a nervous breakdown over his son's deployment. I put him in the hospital. We are very isolated in this small town, and at the beginning of the war we were spit on, had our car door keyed and kicked in.

The straw that broke the camel's proverbial back was when my husband went to the grocery store one day and was run off the road by some idiot in a pickup truck because of our antiwar bumper stickers. This was at the beginning of this senseless war, and we had a child over there. My husband came home shaking and crying, a mess, a total mess. He went under fast. He has been diagnosed with clinical depression, as have I, in fact. The whole family is a mess.

I have kept all of my son Michael's emails. Michael told me that when Rumsfeld landed at Abu Ghraib, he and the other grunts there silently protested Rumsfeld. They went into the Internet café and sat down. Michael's words about Rummy? "He had 10 gunships pointed at him to protect him, an armored vehicle, a presidential helicopter, and we all call him a 'pussy.' " You won't see that on the news, but that's where it's at. The soldiers on the ground think Rummy is a pussy. They hate him.

Michael also told us that ONE WEEK after the torture photographs from Abu Ghraib came out, the goddamned place was air-conditioned. Michael said to me, "All the Iraqi people ever wanted was the truth; all they got was lies."

Michael is a good kid. He also told me he has "seen things and heard of things that are bad, so I'm keeping a journal." I know Michael. He would never keep a journal. I'm glad he is. He needs to get what he is seeing and hearing off his chest for his own mental health.

Remember when Bush said, "We are going to demolish Abu Ghraib" in his lame speech? Well, at that time, I was sending care packages to Michael and to his unit. In fact, I had tons of people at DemocraticUnderground.com sending Michael and the rest of his unit packages. It was great—all the kids were getting something, and it was running along smoothly. Then, that idiot Bush says in his speech, "I'm going to tear down Abu Ghraib." Well, Michael wrote to me right away and said, "Don't send any more care packages! Top brass says we are moving south!"

So I stopped sending the care packages and informed all my friends at Democratic Underground to stop. But what do you think happened? I find out that Bush "inserted" that idea without Congressional approval. MORON!!! Now, Michael's unit, that had REALLY COUNTED ON THOSE CARE PACKAGES, didn't get them anymore. I had to hurriedly recontact everyone on Democratic Underground to tell them what was going on and try and re-enlist their help in sending the care packages. . . .

Bush is so out of touch with every soldier and human being and family member of the military involved in this country and this "war" that he could care less how his "statement" affected our family, and the care packages that weren't sent to these kids. I was so angry I couldn't take it anymore.

I am so tired now I can barely take it. Michael missed our birthdays, his birthday. We have only heard from him ONCE by phone. His emails are far and few. He says his unit is being put in "trailers" now, whatever that means.

He wrote and told us one day "92 people injured today, 22 wounded." He said he cannot take another April bombing.

I informed him via email that Sy Hersh was planning on writing an exposé of the previous unit's rape and sodomizing of young children and women at Abu Ghraib so he can be aware of the possibility of publicity that will come out. Because Michael is THERE at Abu Ghraib, I told him to please, please, please be careful. He is a sitting duck. I even wrote Mr. Hersh and asked him to please tell me when *The New Yorker* intends to publish his piece. I need to know. I need to know. I need to warn Michael because the Muslim world will attack Michael, even though he is just a 21-year-old kid caught up in a world of shit caused by a lot of wealthy bastards and neocons who could care less what happens to these kids. Michael represents the United States to them. But Michael isn't a neocon. He's a kid who plays baseball and wants to be cop someday.

The only solace we have as a family is that he is not a Marine at this point. We still walk around forgetting what day it is, what time it is, and we are all in a daze in this family. I write about this on a blog. It's the only way I can release it, get the fear off my chest. And, yes, the whole family is in counseling. We have to be. The stress is sometimes unbearable. Panic attacks, worry, and, what's worse, knowing perfectly well this whole war was a scam—a fraud—and still is. People all over the country have asked me, "If you had believed in it would it make a difference?"

Well, I don't believe in living in denial. Every soldier who died in Iraq died for nothing. Every civilian who died died for nothing. Everyone who was wounded was wounded for nothing. Nothing. Not a goddamned thing.

People speak abstractly about the war because they have no one over there. It consumes you when someone you love is over there. You have to live it every day, every waking moment. Every second. If a bomb goes off in Fallujah, we know our loved one is five miles away. I have watched my husband sit and cry into his hands, cry and cry all day and not know if Michael was okay because the electricity was down near Baghdad.

There is nothing worse than these armchair warriors who spout and mumble about how wonderful the war is, these vacuous idiots who have no kids over there, who make comments with nothing at stake.

Many women I speak with say one thing . . . these kids are dying for nothing.

And it's true. Perhaps it's hard for the U.S. public to wrap their minds around that truth. Our children have been sent to a war to die for nothing. I knew the truth from the beginning. That made it hard for my husband and me. We were not in denial. We knew about the Carlyle Group, and PNAC, and all of it. We knew. We tried to put a face on the soldiers, on the coffins, on the body bags. We tried. No one listened when we marched or spoke out. Remember, we were "a focus group."

I lay in bed for 2 days the other day. I didn't move. I lay there crying after painting a painting of women lying on the ground, their babies under them, dead, with an American flag waving over them, torn, bleeding onto them . . . because that's what I see. The death of the women and children in Iraq, the death of beauty and truth, the death of something honorable and kind, the death of empathy and compassion. That painting had to come out of me and it did, and now I'm tired.

I'm also not alone. Thousands of other families are weary, tired, alone, wishing to God this was over, wishing their children weren't there, wishing we could make this nightmare go away.

There is a bitter vindication in knowing my husband and I were right all along about this fake war. Bitter. Too many died, too many have died and been destroyed for nothing. Michael is standing in Iraq as we speak. It's not over yet.

I guess I have to believe in a God, but I'm not sure what it is. Maybe the God of compassion, empathy, and a gentle heart. I have no idea if America has any of that left at this point. Thank you for allowing me to write.

164

## "MY BROTHER HAD BEEN KILLED IN THE WAR"

FROM: Michelle Sekara
SENT: Monday, July 12, 2004 9:33 PM
TO: mike@michaelmoore.com
SUBJECT: My brother was a Marine; your movie gave me and my family a voice

I don't know how to write the words I need to write to you in the profound way that I feel them. . . .

Let me first say this . . . you have lifted the unheard, unsung voices of my dead brother, our mother, our sister, my immediate family, and me. . . . I can't say how grateful I am to you for making the movie *Fahrenheit 9/11*.

My brother, Staff Sergeant Michael R. Conner, USMC, was a career soldier initially by "choice" (read: desperation with patriotism) and later by necessity. I once asked him what he really loved and he said, "This," and looked around and said, "America." As you were able to convey in your film, the people who join the Marines are the disenfranchised, the uneducated, the poor. My brother was all these things, including patriotic.

I just want you to know that I finally feel "validated." My brother was killed in the Gulf War in early 1991. He was the first to die in the San Francisco Bay Area, and I miss him every day. His death left behind two little sons aged seven and eleven and his wife. Their 13th wedding anniversary went uncelebrated a few short months after his death.

In spite of our great loss, I want you to know how extremely happy I feel to have our story heard. You may have interviewed a different mother in *Fahrenheit 9/11* and a different family, but it may well have been mine.

For years I've told people, sometimes strangers, that my

brother died in the war, and I often got the response, "What war, the Vietnam War?" I was shocked and amazed . . . and I was angry . . . very angry. I was angry that Desert Storm was not even brought to the American people on TV . . . the extremely limited footage combined with little informative and useful commentary made it seem that nothing unusual was going on . . . yet my brother had been killed in the war and my world turned upside down.

What was really frustrating and angering was that I lived (and still do) in San Francisco, and many of the people here would simply tune out once they heard that my Marine brother had been killed in the war. . . . All of a sudden they didn't know what to say. A few times people said my brother "deserved" to die because after all, he joined the military "voluntarily." I always wondered if these same people's IQs exceeded that of their shoe sizes . . . and if they were born without normal brain circuitry which enables the emotion of empathy to be felt.

I just had to constantly explain to people how and why my brother joined the Marines and that, yes, he was patriotic, and no, he didn't agree with everything our government did.

Your film has created bridges. People can finally see that the very young men and women who join the Marines (and other military branches) are usually doing so out of circumstance, desperation, and because there are no other ways to make a living.

Another bridge your film created was for the people who protested the wars (in the Gulf and the war in Iraq) and with the military families—something that I've long been trying to do. Both the protesters (including myself) and the families of the military are patriotic and express their patriotism by dissenting when they learn that something is not right.

I want to extend an eternal thank-you for illustrating how the world really is . . . for elucidating that our military is not the enemy, but filled with the common "people" and for putting the blame where it rightfully belongs, to Bush and his administration.

The culprits of 9/11 are Bin Laden and al Qaeda, and Bush is still not intent on finding, imprisoning, and punishing them. Bush managed to trick the American people into linking the horrible tragedy of 9/11 to Iraq when no such link exists. This was how he sold the Iraq War to us . . . what a disgrace, what a shame, and what a waste of human lives.

It's clear that the Bush administration cares only for themselves (the superrich and powerful) and not for the rest of America, the common people.

## "Support Our Troops, Dump Bush"

From: Tiffany Benitez
Sent: Thursday, July 15, 2004 4:35 AM
To: mike@michaelmoore.com
Subject: A concerned American

Dear Michael Moore & Readers,

I am a registered nurse in one of the top military hospitals in the country. I work on the ortho floor, which means we get most of the wounded soldiers. We treat injuries having to do with arms, legs, burns, and so forth.

When the war first began, I, like most Americans, thought, All right, we're defending our country against the 9/11 attacks. I am not a Republican, and I never cared for George W. Bush because I never understood how someone who spoke so poorly could be the leader of our country. However, I was quite impressed with the way he took the initiative to defend our country.

In the beginning, the soldiers were coming back, and they all said the same things. "I gotta get back there and take care of my troops," or "I got a job to finish over there, I can't wait to get back." I mean, there were 19-, 20-year-old guys losing arms and legs and saying they would do it all over again if they had to.

As time progressed, their sentiments changed. Now, they are coming back and all saying the same thing. "We're a bunch of sitting ducks over there," or "We don't know what the hell is going on anymore." Just like the corporal in *Fahrenheit 9/11*, these soldiers are saying the same things: they would rather face jail time than go back.

People here at the hospital are debating the movie. Republicans bash it, even though no one I talk to who bashes it has even seen it! Everyone is up in arms over whether Bush is a greedy, manipulative person, and I and a lot of people know he is.

However, when you take all of that away, we are still left with these soldiers. They are young, and now damaged because of this war. A war we did not have to fight! It is so difficult to go to work every day and see soldiers with missing limbs, and see them talking on the telephone to their young girlfriends, knowing they can't possibly understand the impact these injuries and this war will have on their lives. They can't—they are too young to know.

I now have a bumper sticker on my car that says, "Support Our Troops, Dump Bush." By getting rid of Bush, maybe we can eventually get out of Iraq. I live in Texas, and I am so afraid Bush will win again. I would be devastated because I know it means I will be very busy at work, busy treating more injured soldiers. Besides, even if Bush doesn't win, it won't matter because he will just steal the election again!

## "They Can't Send Both Parents to War"

From: Mama Yaa Aseda Hogue
Sent: Tuesday, June 29, 2004 11:02 PM
To: mike@michaelmoore.com
Subject: Your movie should be a "must-see" for Americans

My eldest son, SPC Nathaniel (21 years old) and his wife, SPC Amanda (20 years old) have both been in Tikrit, Iraq, since February 2004. Nathan and HIS WIFE? Mandy left a daughter who is just 14 months old, with us in Oakland, California. They have missed her first steps, her first tooth, her first birthday (April 9, 2004), and her first real words.

When they return, I want to send the U.S. Army a bill for the psychotherapy the whole family will require to rebond their relationships. My son is African American, and Mandy is Mexican American. They wanted to get the college benefits so they joined the army after high school. (Mandy in El Paso, Texas and Nathan in Accokeek, Maryland.) They met, fell in love, and married in the army. God is blessing them to be at the same base in Iraq even though they are in different companies.

When I tell people about my son and daughter-in-law being in Iraq, the first response is, "They can't send both parents to war." The answer is that the U.S. Army can and will do whatever they want as long as the people are in the dark.

Thank God for your movie! At last a blind has been lifted at the White House, and we can see that inside is dirty and broken down. Send the Bush twins over to serve and send my kids home. Thank you for allowing me a place to share my story and vent. I will be helping to get folks to the polls and to your movie.

## "It's Not Enough to Say You Support the Troops"

FROM: Emily Riggs
SENT: Sunday, December 21, 2003 4:58 PM
TO: mike@michaelmoore.com
SUBJECT: Thank you

Dear Mike,

My husband got out of the army in February just before most of the men in his unit were deployed to Iraq.

I cannot express to you enough how much I agree with your statement about how our "president" is the one who really does not support the troops. I have grown up around the military my entire life. My father was an army captain, and my husband was a sergeant when he got out. Military families are forced to sacrifice so much for so little. My children rarely got to spend a Christmas or a birthday with their father, and when he was sent to Korea for a year, we were not only on our own but we had to make due with less money because they took away his separate rations. That is how much appreciation the government has for the job these guys do.

My husband, not unlike countless others who join the armed services, only joined because they promised him a free college education, which he is now taking advantage of. But it was far from free. He spent ten years of his life working long hours for VERY little pay and even less appreciation.

I would like to express to people that it is not enough just to say that you support our troops. You should lobby your congressmen and -women to support a pay raise for the troops and support initiatives to build newer, better quality housing for military families. And most of all, if you really support the troops, you should insist that they be brought home NOW and that this meaningless war come to an end as soon as possible before more of the people they "support" are killed or wounded.

## "I CHECK MY EMAIL ALL DAY, EVERY DAY"

FROM: Anonymous
SENT: Tuesday, July 6, 2004 3:12 PM
TO: mike@michaelmoore.com
SUBJECT: When is my husband coming home?

Dear Michael,

My friends and I just saw *Fahrenheit 9/11*, and I want to say thank you. I applaud you for showing people the proof of what our country is doing.

My husband is serving in the army and has been gone since January of this year. They told him he would be gone 12 months. I received his first letter in February, when they actually started counting their 12 months, to tell me that he will be gone 18 months. They also canceled their leave for this year, so we don't know when we will see him at all. We email each other, and he tries to call when he is able to. We have two toddlers, and I reassure them all the time that their dad loves them and that his job is very hard, so we may not see him for a long time.

I cry all the time because I receive emails from all the other wives who are losing their husbands. My kids rely on pictures and postcards to hear from their father, and I check my email all day, every day, to see if he has written. I miss my husband.

Thank you for the truth and for showing the pain that comes with war. Thank you so much for pissing a lot of people off with the truth.

## "He Has Taken My Child from Me"

From: Nancy W.
Sent: Friday, July 2, 2004 2:04 AM
To: mike@michaelmoore.com
Subject: Stop the war! Bring my child home ALIVE

Dear Mr. Moore,

I have seen *Fahrenheit 9/11* several times. Each showing has made me angrier and angrier at the situation we Americans have allowed to occur under the Bushwhacker. I was particularly moved by the Flint, Michigan, mom who lost her son in this senseless conflict. I told my children many of the same things she told her children. I encouraged my daughter and son to join the military, see the world, learn a trade, and have money for college. What a fool I was!

My oldest daughter is in the Marines and is being sent to the hellhole of the world, Iraq—even though the war is over. She went into the Marines because I was a single mom, with the inability to pay her way through college. What of the world has she seen? Okinawa for the past 14 months, and now she is being sent to Iraq for an unknown period of time. As she told me, she's just a fresh piece of meat to be ground up in the "war." It will be anywhere from 24 months to 32 months before I see her again and can hold her close.

I have been against not only the war but Bush himself, but now that he has taken my child from me, I am fighting mad. She will never be the same after going there. Outwardly she may look the same, but her spirit and soul will be forever changed. I want to march, carry a sign to "Bring the troops home," or speak against Bush, but I feel there is no place for me in my country.

Keep your message coming forth—keep it coming for those of us who have no platform from which to express our views. Thank you for the message in *Fahrenheit 9/11*.

## "THEY HAVE ACCUSED HIM OF COWARDICE"

FROM: Anonymous
SENT: Wednesday, July 7, 2004 5:16 PM
TO: mike@michaelmoore.com
SUBJECT: Marine mom against the war

Just saw *Fahrenheit 9/11*. It made me weep. Last year, my son and I were featured in a series of articles in the *Chicago Tribune* because I was protesting the war while he was fighting it.

He killed a civilian woman his first week in Iraq and didn't have the stomach to fight after that incident. Last fall, he was given an honorable discharge from the Marine Corps, and is prohibited from ever reenlisting.

They have accused him of cowardice. I think he is simply human. The emotional effects of killing innocent people are another by-product of this needless war.

You have done an enormous service to military families everywhere by demonstrating the horrors of war, its brutalizing effect on our troops, and the innocent people we kill in the name of "freeing" them.

## "Trouble Isn't Trouble
Until It Visits One's Own Home"

FROM: M.G.M.
SENT: Monday, July 12, 2004 9:13 PM
TO: mike@michaelmoore.com
SUBJECT: Your movie

Mike,

As a mother of a young soldier who recently completed an enlistment, I was taken by your movie. I was especially touched by the loss the family felt in the death of their son. My child served four years with an additional three months added to the agreed upon enlistment.

The dilemma our family faces now is that our child may be called up again for additional time to go to Iraq or Afghanistan to serve out the "inactive reserve" portion of the contract, which was not explained at the time of signing. I canNOT relate to the recruiters signing these young people up to serve with a dishonest intent. It just grieves my entire spirit to see these young people being forced to fight a war that has no justification other than greed.

It is like sending "hogs" off to slaughter as many, many of them will never return, and most will never be the same after their ordeals. My 23-year-old has experienced more emotional horror than I could ever imagine in my 45 years of life. There is such trauma associated with this ordeal that only God can restore.

I am in touch with many of my child's friends who served alongside each other while in active duty and during a tour to the Middle East shortly after 9/11. Their whole mentality is not what normal early 20-year-olds should be dealing with. Many of them grieve for their friends, and it is not unusual to see them with tattoos bearing the initials R.I.P. with dedications to their fallen comrades on their bodies. This just breaks my heart. I am sure the thought has not occurred to Bush that for every member of the armed services who is "murdered" in the Middle East, there are many people who are connected to that one person. I appreciated the part of the movie that showed the members of Congress who were not willing to sacrifice their own children. That was really worth highlighting. You see, trouble isn't trouble until it visits one's own home.

I am encouraging every person I know to vote Bush out of office in November. This is the only hope for the world as we have known it and the only chance for some resemblance of peace. As a Christian, it is difficult for me to see Bush as a man of God as I've heard from so many pundits throughout the country, and the world for that matter. I respect his position as the president, though he was not my choice. However, pain, destruction, and chaos are all that have come from his presidency for ordinary people, which has hindered many of us from accomplishing extraordinary things.

George W. Bush has only brought about very bad things that have hurt so many people. That is a direct opposition of what God would want for people. It's a sad day in our nation if George W. Bush is allowed to continue his destructive and deviant behavior for four more years. I for one thank God for your documentary. It has been revelation for me and I hope for others.

## "I HAVE BEEN WORKING NONSTOP TO STOP THIS WAR"

FROM: Nancy Brown
SENT: Friday, July 9, 2004 11:38 AM
TO: mike@michaelmoore.com
SUBJECT: From an MFSO member with a son in Iraq

Dear Michael Moore,

My son Ryan is a member of the Vermont National Guard who signed up for tuition money before the war started. Never did he dream he would be in mortal danger driving a Humvee in Baghdad and its surroundings (sometimes on RPG Alley).

He tells me he will be voting against Bush.

I have been working nonstop to stop this war, using my personal experience to get more and more members to join Military Families Speak Out (www.mfso.org). I have been speaking on local TV and radio stations, going to rallies and panel discussions.

From the bottom of my heart, thank you for what you are doing to help my son, all the other soldiers, and the Iraqi people—indeed, to help America extricate herself from this mess.

## "I Cried When She Left"

From: C.S.
Sent: Sunday, July 4, 2004 6:40 PM
To: mike@michaelmoore.com
Subject: Thank you

Dear Mr. Moore,

Yesterday, Saturday, July 3rd, my wife deployed for training in Fort Bliss, Texas. She is part of the HHC, for the 116th Engineer Battalion, Idaho Army National Guard. She is to spend roughly two months in Texas, then her unit is being sent to Fort Polk, Louisiana. There she will continue to train until November, before being sent to Iraq.

I cried when she left yesterday. I cried and I held our two sons close to me. They are both too young to understand what is going on, but in a little while they will be able to ask me where Mommy is. Watching my wife board that bus was one of the hardest things that I have ever had to do. I, too, was in the Idaho Army National Guard, for four and a half years. As a matter of fact, that is where we met.

I watched *Fahrenheit 9/11* today, and I cried again. To hear Mrs. Lipscomb talk about the loss of her son made me think about what I would do if I lost my wife. I can honestly say I don't know how I would react if it did happen.

I admit that I was one of the millions of Americans who voted for George W. Bush back in 2000, because of his lies. I wish I hadn't. Idaho is primarily a Republican state, so I think that, once again, Bush will win it in 2004. It is probably one of the few states where Bush actually did win the electoral vote.

I think back to the founding of our great country, and how in a presidential election, the winner became president, and the loser became vice president. We do live in fictitious times, with a fictitious leader. A regular "commander in thief." I know for a fact that all of my family, who are primarily Republican, are not going to vote for Bush this election. Please continue to make good movies, and show the American people, as well as the world, about the injustice being done in the name of good.

## "THERE SHE WAS, LEFT ALONE"

FROM: Eric Morrison
SENT: Sunday, December 21, 2003 5:02 PM
TO: mike@michaelmoore.com
SUBJECT: Little brother back from Iraq

Hey Michael,

My younger brother just got out of the Marines and was one of the first to hit the ground when the war started. It was probably the scariest time of my life having to watch the biased news coverage of the preemptive invasion and wondering every moment where my brother was. I was struck with guilt, feeling that it should have been me over there instead of him. There were a lot of emotions, and I could go on for a long time about this, but there is one story that I would like to share with you that will only take a minute, as it is something I will not forget for the rest of my life.

After Bush declared the war officially over, my brother was lucky to be one of the first units to leave as they had seen some of the heaviest action. I spent the summer backpacking Europe, but on my way over from Alaska I first stopped in North Carolina to welcome home my brother and the rest of his buddies.

It was a great feeling to see him after the whole ordeal and to be able to give him a big hug and tell him I love him. Right after the buses pulled into the Marine base, I noticed a group of Marines standing in a single-file line, and I was wondering what they were doing, since they had just stepped off the bus.

I watched as each Marine, having just spent months in hell, and before they spent time with their families or friends, each of them paid their respects to the family of a fallen Marine. The mother of this fallen soldier was sitting on the edge of a grass field at the unit's barracks, the father standing beside her, and each Marine proceeded to give her a hug and then shake the father's hand.

I stood there transfixed and watched as about 30 Marines did this, unable to avert my watery eyes. Then the last one gave her a hug and there she was, left alone. It was without a doubt the saddest moment I have ever witnessed, and it made me sick to my stomach. It filled me with guilt that I was experiencing so much joy by the return of my brother and someone else was breathing the same air I was, yet experiencing so much sorrow.

The soldier who died was one of the AAV drivers killed near Nasiriyah right around the same time Jessica Lynch's ordeal happened. I really enjoyed the recent newsletter of yours and how you said that it is important to say you support the troops even though you oppose the war. Well, I opposed the war and saw right through the lies, but I had no choice but to support my kid brother and his brothers in arms.

My brother is now retired from the Marines and is stuck in the lackluster economy of Oregon searching for a suitable job. The fucked-up part is that even though he put his life on the line in the Middle East in 2001, and again in Iraq in 2003, the only job he could get to pay his bills is as a seasonal telemarketer for a big southern Oregon fruit corporation.

I'm not sure how many people will have sent in emails regarding this, but he loves movies and if you can put him on that list for a copy of *Bowling for Columbine*, I'd be very grateful. Sorry this was so long, but I had a few things I wanted to tell you.

## "I'M ALREADY GOING CRAZY,
## PRAYING HE WILL COME HOME"

FROM: Metta Switalski
SENT: Tuesday, July 6, 2004 2:35 AM
TO: mike@michaelmoore.com
SUBJECT: My story

Hi. My name is Metta Switalski. My husband is in the army and is stationed in Korea, for now. We reenlisted for Korea for 18 months to prevent him from going to Iraq, but the day he left was the day they announced that they would be sending 3,600 soldiers from Korea to Iraq. I prayed so hard that he wouldn't be one of the too many being sent over there, but he is. He will be going in August.

I know in my heart that he will come home, but I have come to terms with what could happen over there.

I don't claim to know what the government is doing to this country or what we are really doing in Iraq. Because I think that if I really knew what my husband is doing I would go crazy. I'm already going crazy just praying that he will come home and knowing that the day he left could be the last time I get to see him. I'm not a religious person by any means, but I think in my own way that I am now.

I don't know why I decided to write to you and tell you my story, but thank you for taking the time to read it. I also want to thank you for everything you do for the men and women in the military and for their families. Being a military wife, it means a lot to me that there are people like you who actually care what happens to us and who are trying to make a difference.

## "HIS NAME IS MARCUS"

FROM: M. Denton
SENT: Monday, December 22, 2003 11:44 AM
TO: mike@michaelmoore.com
SUBJECT: My brother the soldier

Mr. Moore,

I don't know why I am writing to you. Maybe it's just so that I can tell you a little bit about my brother who is serving over in Mosul, Iraq.

His name is Marcus. We call him Mark. Or if you're family, we call him Marky. He's 20. He joined the army straight out of high school. He actually had to wait a couple weeks after graduation to sign up. That is when he turned 18. My sister is his twin. He was at Fort Benning during his phase of boot camp when 9/11 occurred. It was also at this time I found out that my brother had joined up to be in the infantry. Of course my heart sank. I think he didn't tell me 'cause he knew I probably wouldn't handle it too well. Well, now he is a driver of a Stryker.

Each time I hear of another soldier being wounded or dying in Iraq my heart sinks and I stop breathing. I get angry. I get very angry. I've felt this way since this horrible war started. I wait to hear where it occurred. And if it occurred in Mosul, I simply wait to see if the phone will ring. Even when I haven't heard the latest news, I hate it when my phone rings. I hate it when I can see that a phone call is coming from my home state of California. I'm ALWAYS thinking in the back of my mind, "This is it. This is the call that will break my heart." Thank God that hasn't happened yet. I don't know how the families who have lost their loved ones over in this war can carry on. My heart goes out to them.

I finally saw your documentary *Bowling for Columbine*. I remember that Oscar speech very well.

My mouth dropped open to say the least. Let me explain why. I kept up with what was going on in the world. At least I thought I did. I watched the news. I read the news. I guess being a parent to a then 5-year-old and 2-year-old was keeping me from really learning about the big picture of it all.

I didn't understand why you were saying what you said. The only thing I could gather from your speech was that you were still angry about the election, which I did keep up with when it happened and could understand why you felt the way you did.

I just wanted to say thank you. Thank you for opening my eyes. They were never closed . . . just averted some. I'm a busy lady. But I try to do what I can. The care kits to the Iraqi children have sparked a lot of interest in me, and I think I can get a group to make some up in the near future. I hope I can. If I can't, I'll make some on my own and send them out. My kids need to see their mother helping out children who don't have what they have.

## "There Is Certainly Great Sadness"

FROM: S.L.S.
SENT: Saturday, July 3, 2004 11:10 PM
TO: mike@michaelmoore.com
SUBJECT: Thank you from an air force mom

Dear Michael,

Having seen your film, I would like to thank you for your efforts and particularly for the clip regarding the wounded soldiers.

My daughter is in the air force and stationed in Germany. She and her fiancé, also an airman, recently came home for a visit. As they are both in the medical field, I asked them to share with me their experiences and thoughts about the war in Iraq. They eagerly shared their personal thoughts about the war but also began telling of daily incoming flights filled to capacity with the wounded soldiers from Iraq. As they relayed the numbers I found myself in disbelief that this number was a DAILY occurrence. I grilled them repeatedly, not wanting to believe what I was hearing, that EVERY DAY a plane flew in filled to capacity with wounded, some of whom were on life support.

I shamefully admit that up until their report of this I had not considered the wounded. Yes, as I read the death toll reported daily in the morning paper and on the radio, my sadness each day was momentarily intense. But as with so many of us, the daily responsibilities of my personal life allowed me to push aside this atrocity for the time being and get about my business.

As my daughter and her fiancé shared more, I was aghast to learn that, depending on when a wounded soldier dies (i.e., after leaving Iraq or in flight out of Iraq) they may or MAY NOT be counted as a casualty of war, suggesting that the numbers we are privy to via the news media do not reflect the actual count. True to my form, I was outraged and questioned why there was no news coverage about this. Where were the journalists, who once went to great efforts in trying to figure out where President Clinton did what with whom and a cigar?

I was reminded of a story one of my coworkers had shared about her son, a military man recently home from Iraq. I had in fact sent a letter to the editor of our local newspaper relaying the story and asking why more wasn't written on the trauma these soldiers come home with (I received no response from the paper).

There is certainly great sadness for all of our fine young men and women who go forth under the guise of protecting us, only to lose their lives by so doing. That we might fail to acknowledge the number of soldiers whose lives will never be the same because of mental trauma or physical wounds is shameful and cowardly.

Interestingly, and to my pleasant surprise, my other half, who has been a card-carrying Republican for years, and having done the research for himself, has now made a commitment to do all he can to get Bush out of office. Being a pretty liberal person, I had been working on him and ever so slowly moving him into the light. Your movie was the last little push he needed. I thank you for that.

## "WE ARE SICK OF BEING MANIPULATED AND LIED TO"

FROM: Bob and Heather Sommer
SENT: Sunday, July 4, 2004 11:14 PM
TO: mike@michaelmoore.com
SUBJECT: Thank you!

Dear Michael,

Our son is currently serving in the army in Iraq. We want to thank you for producing this film and bottling all of the rage and frustration that we have experienced in the past year into a couple of hours of superb filmmaking.

Perhaps the greatest testament to your message and its effectiveness is that our soon-to-be-voting-for-the-first-time daughter and many of her friends have been impacted by your film and will be heading for the voting booth in November. We continually grieve for those families who experience the pain that we most fear. This administration is the worst in the history of this country, and we are sick of being manipulated and lied to. Your film has done a great service to our country, and we were proud to see it on the evening of July 4th, in lieu of attending the fireworks!

## "I AM OUTRAGED"

FROM: Carrie Philpott
SENT: Tuesday, July 6, 2004 11:06 AM
TO: mike@michaelmoore.com
SUBJECT: Making medical scrubs for military doctors in Baghdad

Dear Mr. Moore,

I am writing to you today to inform you of something that I find appalling beyond words.

I am a Marine Corps mother whose 19-year-old son is currently stationed in Iraq. This is not an "honor" that I wear on my sleeve, but I feel that it is important to support and aid our troops as I can. I became acquainted with a woman whose army reservist son is currently serving as a medical doctor at one of the U.S. Army hospitals in Baghdad. We share our fears for our sons whenever she frequents my place of work.

Two weeks ago she mentioned that she would be making medical scrubs for her son and some of the other doctors and medics because they are not being supplied with an adequate number of scrub uniforms to have sterile garb for each shift of work. She asked if I would be willing to help make scrubs. I am a professional individual in the sewing-related business and was thrilled to spend my days off helping in any way I could. The last thing I would want is for my son to be injured on the battlefield and the attending doctor and hospital not to be an adequately sterile environment.

I am outraged that the U.S. government, with all of the contract money being allocated for war efforts, is not able to find the money to budget for these necessary supplies. I believe that this is an area of expenditure (or lack of) that needs immediate investigation. Are you up for it?

## "TODAY HE IS FLYING BACK TO IRAQ"

FROM: Patricia LaRue
SENT: Saturday, July 10, 2004 6:19 AM
TO: mike@michaelmoore.com
SUBJECT: Thank you for the truth

I am a mother of a soldier who has been in Iraq, and although he has been back in the States for the last five months, today he is flying back to Iraq. I have been shocked and stunned that he was ever sent there at all. The army recruiter virtually guaranteed that my son would NOT be asked to serve in the war zone. My son is the ONLY surviving son to carry on the family name, and his dad is deceased. In my son rests the entire future of our family line.

Initially, I tried to support Bush. I listened carefully to all the news, from every source, and analyzed the discussions as new events developed. In the end, the conclusion I arrived at was one that was in conflict with my support for my son. I had to resolve this conflict quickly, for the sake of my son. So my support for my son as a soldier and as my son became distinct from my opposition to the war and to Bush's policies. Nevertheless, this does not help in any way to ameliorate my worries about my son's safety.

I contacted the army about my son's status as sole surviving son. I was told that the prior policy of protecting such soldiers was changed during the Gulf War (under Bush-daddy). In other words, neither Bush gives a rat's *** about such Americans whose sacrifice may end their family name forever, who have the least in support networks (i.e., I have no husband to share the burden of the worry with).

I just want you to know that my youngest daughter and I saw the film today. Almost everything you presented were things we knew or suspected; but you connected all the dots in a way that made it understandable.

## "A REAL PATRIOT"

FROM: Terry LeBlanc
SENT: Wednesday, July 7, 2004 7:47 AM
TO: mike@michaelmoore.com
SUBJECT: Thank you

I just want to let you know you saved a life. My 19-year-old son has been planning to join the ROTC in college because he wants to be a "real" patriot. He signed up for their course this fall. No amount of begging, rationalization or bribes were working to prevent him from signing up.

Then the other day he went to see *Fahrenheit 9/11*. He came home and announced he was totally changing his mind and recognized he could be patriotic in other ways, i.e., being an informed voter. The words don't exist to express my gratitude to you.

## "It's Easy to Profess Patriotism"

FROM: S.C.
SENT: Monday, December 29, 2003 12:01 PM
TO: mike@michaelmoore.com
SUBJECT: Thank you, Mr. Moore

On December 6th, my organization was a part of the holiday family-support meeting of one of our local National Guard units. Eight volunteers and their therapy animals went to the meeting in hopes of providing a little nontraditional holiday cheer to some folks who are facing hard times.

Most of the unit members had recently returned from bases in Texas and Virginia, where they had been filling spots vacated by active-duty members of the military who had been deployed to the Middle East. These same Guard members had also just learned that they will be redeployed in the coming months to serve again, this time in Iraq.

I sat on the floor with my dog and talked with kids of all ages and parents who were putting on brave faces. I found it difficult to breathe for a moment when I realized that I was in the company of moms and dads who may leave for a country halfway across the globe in a few months and never come home again.

But the face I remember most clearly from that meeting belonged to a uniformed man who came in with his four-year-old son. I watched him as he watched his boy, and I could see the man committing every detail to memory, trying to wring every ounce of sweetness and clarity from the moment. He was present, every quiet breath filled with purpose and a pleasure so simple it was almost painful to see.

I live in a section of the country that is strongly conservative, Republican, and very supportive of the current administration. To oppose the war in Iraq in my town—or to say anything critical regarding any aspect of this administration's policies or performance—is about as close to blasphemy as you can get. Those of us who do, do so quietly.

I'm angry that I am accused of a lack of patriotism by people who plant a flag in their front yard and park their SUV—a vehicle that only accelerates our dependence on foreign oil—in the drive next to it. I am amazed and appalled that they claim support of the men and women dying in Iraq for our "freedom," but acknowledge no connection between their decisions and lifestyle choices and the real reason for those men and women to be in harm's way.

It's easy to profess patriotism and love of country from a stool at the local pub, fortified by a pint or two, when you aren't inconvenienced by sleeping in a sandy foxhole thousands of miles from family, friends, and everything familiar to you. It's easy to be patriotic when there's no chance CNN might startle you with the image of a series of flag-draped coffins being unloaded from the belly of a military transport plane because your president has ordered that those images not be publicly broadcast.

George W. Bush is perfectly willing to stand on the deck of the USS *Lincoln* and be filmed and photographed with living GIs for broadcast on the evening news, but he has no interest in broadcasting their images once they've died for our country.

## "I Had No Answer for Him"

FROM: Sherri Davis
SENT: Sunday, July 4, 2004 3:42 PM
TO: mike@michaelmoore.com
SUBJECT: None

Michael,

I am a mother whose daughter just got out of the military. She was blessed in that she had just left Korea when her whole unit got orders to ship out for Iraq in August. Her fiancé went in August. She recently got a call from the Reserves saying that her number is on their list to call should we need "BACK UP." Since she put in less than eight years, she still can be called in to duty at any time.

I went to see your film. It confirmed everything I thought about him and his administration. I am so glad someone has finally come out and told the truth in a manner that will make everyone sit up and take notice! Michael, from all of the military Moms I want to thank you. When I saw you go up to Congress members and ask if they wanted their kids to go off to war, it was PRICELESS! The looks on their faces! I wanted to scream at them "YES, BUT IT'S OK FOR MY CHILD TO DEFEND YOU."

My 15-year-old son summed it up best. He said, "Mom, if they tried to impeach President Clinton for lying about who he slept with, why aren't they impeaching Bush for all the LIES he told?" I HAD NO ANSWER FOR HIM!

## "MY FATHER BEARS THE SCARS OF WAR"

FROM: C. Harned
SENT: Sunday, March 7, 2004 11:45 PM
TO: mike@michaelmoore.com
SUBJECT: Thoughts to ponder

Dear Mr. Moore,

I am Left in a family of Rights and am always trying to get my point across, usually unsuccessfully. However, this Bush military "question" may be just the thing to trip them up.

My point is that my father was a Vietnam vet, and he served his time, got malaria, served some more, and came home. I am sure that this is a typical story. However, I am equally sure that my father suffered "fall outs" throughout his life, as many others did. I grew up with a man who was deeply disturbed with his role in the Vietnam conflict which made for, or contributed to, a rather dysfunctional family life. I watched my father eat leftovers from the fridge that were way past their prime so that he was not wasting food, and heaven forbid if I used a paper towel just to dry my hands in a time when his economic situation did not call for such extreme measures.

My father spoke of the women and children in Vietnam begging for food at the gates and giving them what he could spare of his rations. He was never the same. And he heard and saw men, or shall I say boys, such as himself, crying for their mothers when a bomb hit a tent, and he came home unable to communicate to his family yet desperately needing their support and finding they were unable to give it. For who can assuage a conscience that underwent so many terrors and guilt? And my father was one of the "lucky ones"; he just called in the air strikes, he wasn't on the ground fighting.

While my father, and many like him, bear the scars of being in a war, Bush gets time off during an election campaign, among other "leaves" from "action." If only the masses could be as fortunate as President Bush. It is utterly contemptible.

I don't have a voice to push issues such as these, but you do, and I suggest that somebody get on the bandwagon and point these things out to the American people. Unfortunately, people only vote for an individual because of a few issues—make this one of them.

And for God's sake, court the poor and lower classes, they are the ones truly affected (at least negatively) by all that Bush stands for. I'm willing to stand outside a welfare office and tell them what their options are. And how about some funding for carpools or other forms of transportation to get to those polling booths? Just brainstorming.

## "CARRYING A SIGN, 'SOLDIER AGAINST THE WAR'"

FROM: Susan Neumann
SENT: Saturday, June 26, 2004
TO: mike@michaelmoore.com
SUBJECT: Thank you

I am the grandmother of a 23-year-old soldier who joined the army when he was a senior in high school for the usual reason: to get a college education. So far he has not been educated in Bosnia for one year, South Korea for another year, and various U.S. bases. He currently is in New York, flies the Blackhawk helicopter, and is hoping to be discharged in June 2005, at his required 6-year term.

Many of the soldiers he knows have been extended due to the "stop-gap" measure, and his roommate is on his way to Iraq now. He is totally against this unjust war, and has stood at several war protests, including New York City, carrying a sign, "Soldier Against the War." He does not appear in uniform at these protests.

I wish every citizen was required to view your movie before they were allowed to vote.

## "WHAT KIND OF NAME IS 'HASSAN'?"

FROM: Alicia Sulok
SENT: Saturday, July 31, 2004 5:00 PM
TO: mike@michaelmoore.com
SUBJECT: None

My dad's name is Farouk Diab. He is a veteran of the U.S. Army, and he was a hero in the Korean War. This year while traveling to New Mexico, my father was stopped by airport security. The sad fact is that he was stopped not once but three times on separate occasions! He wasn't stopped because of his record or because of his status in this country. He has been a United States citizen ever since he fought for the U.S. in the Korean War. His only fault was he used his legal name of Farouk instead of Frank, which he usually goes by. Every time he told the security people he was an American and proud of it, but he also told them he was a Muslim who fought for the civil liberties that every American enjoys today.

My father raised us to be proud of our American heritage and at the same time to love our religion as much as our country. My dad loved President Eisenhower and has voted Republican since 1950 when he could first vote.

But he's voting for Kerry and casting a Democratic vote for the first time, thanks to this administration's racist policies and prejudice, which also includes a beating of my Uncle Allen Hassan, who is a Vietnam vet, U.S. Marine. Uncle Hassan actually volunteered for military service in 1964 and returned to duty as a medic in 1969.

Recently, he was arrested when a state trooper asked him what kind of name "Hassan" is. When my uncle responded it was an Arabic name, the trooper pulled him forcefully out of the car and put him in a choke hold. My uncle, who was 66 at the time, felt his breathing was at jeopardy and pushed the officer aside. He woke up naked in a jail cell with 3 cracked ribs and a punctured lung. All of this because he was on his way to the emergency room, where he has been saving lives since 1973. He was speeding, but his crime was that his dad was born in Jerusalem in 1910.

His father was a Muslim, and his last name was Hassan. Even he voted Republican. There are over 7 million Muslims in America and 90% are Republicans. I can guarantee one thing: Bush and his administration will not win the election. All the Muslims I know who are American are mortified at this Nazilike administration.

May God bless you, Michael. You understand what believing in God is all about. It's about fighting for injustice whenever you see it, not just saying you love this country but standing up for what's right and speaking out against lies and ignorance. That's what makes a true believer in God and in this great country of ours. Let's keep it that way. God bless all of the righteous all over the world who want what Jesus, Moses, and Mohammed wanted: Justice for all!

## "WE SAT IN STUNNED SILENCE, UNABLE TO MOVE"

FROM: Christine Davila
SENT: Monday, July 12, 2004 10:50 PM
TO: mike@michaelmoore.com
SUBJECT: Fort Bragg soldier views "9/11"

I have seen *Fahrenheit 9/11* twice, each time taking different people with me. I am writing to tell you about my first visit to see the movie.

I went with my 20-year-old son (whose name is Michael) and his 19-year-old friend, who is a Fort Bragg soldier. I can only say that at the end of the movie all three of us sat in stunned silence unable to move.

After a few minutes we walked in silence to the car, and as we approached our vehicle my son broke down sobbing in grief. He hugged his friend and they both cried, and my son apologized to his friend for a country that will be sending him into harm's way come this December, which is when he is scheduled to leave for Iraq.

During the drive home we did not say much, but I could see my son's friend in the backseat deep in thought, his young eyes filled with hurt and concern. I did talk with both of them about using their greatest freedom, the freedom to vote. But our current leadership (or rather lack of) has left our young people with so much lack of trust. They lack trust in our ability to protect them, and they even lack trust in our electoral system. I do, however, believe that your brave movie has lifted them up and has given them the spark and energy to work toward making sure a change takes place in November.

## "There Is No Way I'm Joining Now"

FROM: T.E.
SENT: Monday, July 5, 2004 9:23 PM
TO: mike@michaelmoore.com
SUBJECT: Lubbock, Texas

I took my 17-year-old daughter and her 18-year-old boyfriend to *Fahrenheit 9/11* on Saturday, July 3, here in Lubbock, Texas. As we waited in line outside, we were laughing at the fact that someone had vandalized the sign outside the theater advertising your movie. My daughter's boyfriend has been determined to join the military as soon as he graduated from high school this summer. I have been talking to him about this pathetic war, to no avail.

The theater was so crowded that we had to sit across the theater from each other, so I couldn't gauge his response during the film. Needless to say, I was very anxious to see him afterward. As soon as we reached the outside door, he came bounding up to me and said, "You just saved my life, there is no way I'm joining now." I wanted to cry; I was so proud to have made a difference in his life by taking him to see your movie. Thank you for taking the heat for all of us who just want the truth.

## "My Brother Would Have
## Preferred a Quick Death"

FROM: Annemarie Wicks
SENT: Wednesday, May 5, 2004 11:39 PM
TO: mike@michaelmoore.com
SUBJECT: Soldiers' suicides

Michael,

First of all, thank you for including those soldiers who've died in
this "war" over in Iraq. My question for you, however, revolves
around the military suicides, both those in combat and by those
soldiers who kill themselves after coming back to the States due to
post-traumatic stress disorder. My brother, Marine SGT Boyd W.
"Chip" Wicks Jr., a member of the one out of five Marines who
saw some of the first fighting in Baghdad, was honorably discharged in October of 2003 after serving his 4 years. He suffered
from extreme PTSD, but refused to get help even after several attempts by his friends and family to get him counseling. He told
my mom three days before he died that the commandante who
spoke to them upon leaving Iraq and arriving in Kuwait told them
not to go home acting like crybabies and complaining of PTSD—
that they were to go to a bar and "tie one on" with friends and
that's how they were to deal with the horrors they endured. On
February 23, 2004, my brother hung himself in his apartment.
He was found after his heart had already stopped; he was revived,
and was in a trauma ICU at Christiana Hospital in Wilmington,
Delaware. After being told he would never regain brain function
enough to survive off the vent, we, as a family, decided to termi-
nally wean him. My brother was full of life and touched a lot of
lives, as is shown by the 600+ folks who came to his viewing. His

unit was awarded a Presidential Honor and he was awarded an individual presidential medal for heroism for acts during the Iraq War. Surely, these soldiers who've committed suicide due to the emotional hell that this war has caused are just as much casualties as those who've died from bombs or gunshot wounds. I think my brother would've preferred a quick death due to a bullet to the heart than the emotional hell that he endured for months after leaving the frontlines.

Thank you,
Annemarie Wicks

# Epilogue

# Letter from Abdul Henderson

*Decorated Marine Lance Corporal Abdul Henderson's principled deci-*
*sion to refuse any future orders to return to Iraq under threat of jail time*
*is born of his conviction that the war being waged there is an unjust one.*
*Lance Corporal Henderson embodies a unique and instructive courage.*
*His story is featured in* Fahrenheit 9/11.

It is an honor to be asked by Mr. Moore to share my thoughts and feelings. I would first like to say that I am not anti-war or anti-military service. It's also been an even bigger honor to be able to contribute the last five years of my life to defending the United States of America. That is what I felt I was doing by appearing in *Fahrenheit 9/11*, defending the United States. It is my civic duty as a Marine and a citizen to protect the Constitution and the sanctity of democracy.

No soldier ever dies in vain in war, if it is justified or not. A soldier's willingness to sacrifice his life for a larger cause is a self-less act and a very humble one indeed. A soldier dies in vain only when the citizens of America don't partake in the political process by not voting. The very essence of democracy is the vote! The ability to pick and choose the leaders of the United States is what we die and fight for. Most countries in the world don't have that ability and would love to be able to simply cast a vote and truly pick their leaders.

People who don't vote for one reason or another do a disservice to the men and women in uniform who protect that right and other rights that are provided to citizens under the Constitution. Every now and then the process seems to have broken, and corruption is very evident, but it is the vote that is to provide the checks and balances. If the vast majority of Americans don't take the time to vote or take the time to understand the political process, we will find that more situations like the war in Iraq will occur.

The war in Iraq is unwarranted and the costs are too high for the American people. We are spending a billion dollars a week to rebuild and secure a country that was no "imminent threat" to America. It is sad to say that there are some places in Iraq that are more secure than some places in America. We are spending a billion dollars a week to rebuild Iraq's educational infrastructure when there are students across America who can't take home books to do homework. We are spending a billion dollars a week to rebuild Iraq's health-care infrastructure when America's elderly and children don't have any health-care coverage. Just imagine if we spent a billion dollars a week to rebuild America's schools and neighborhoods.

The war rhetoric before Operation Iraqi Freedom began was that Saddam Hussein was an imminent threat to America and that he has weapons of mass destruction. From my experience in Iraq and my understanding of imminent threats like the Germans and the Japanese during World War II, the Chinese during the Korean War, and communist Russia during the cold war, Iraq was no imminent threat. Threats of this magnitude fight until there is no one else standing. They don't leave entire tank divisions abandoned in the desert like the Iraqis did. Soldiers don't bring handbags with civilian clothes in them and then change from army fatigues to civilian clothes and then desert their post to return home to their neighborhoods and villages. Imminent threats have a military infrastructure that is sustainable. They don't have buildings that are in ruins like every military installation we occupied in Iraq. And *where* are the weapons of mass destruction?

War should not be waged unless it is absolutely necessary! It is unfair to the men and women of the armed services to have their sense of duty and obligation taken advantage of in an unjust war. Most military personnel will fight and die for this country and not ask a question as to why war is being waged. It is the pride of serving that prevents most soldiers from questioning authority. That's why I joined the Marine Corps, the pride. I didn't join because of necessity. I joined because I wanted to.

As the war in Iraq continues to be waged with no end in sight, I have only one request of the reader, and that is to get involved in the democratic process, understand how our country works, understand who is running our country, and, most important, voice your opinions, even if it's contrary to the nation's leadership. That's what democracy is all about. And don't forget to vote, because the politicians work for you, you don't work for the politicians; hold them accountable for their actions. As Abraham Lincoln once said, "If you give the people the facts, the Republic will be safe."

Abdul R. Henderson

# Appendix

Appendix

## Ways You Can Support Our Troops

Homes for Our Troops
homesforourtroops.org/
Their mission is to build specially adapted homes for our severely disabled soldiers and their families.

The Wounded Warrior Project
unitedspinal.org/pages.php?catid=211&catorder=100
The Wounded Warrior Project seeks to assist those men and women of our armed forces who have been severely injured during the conflicts in Iraq, Afghanistan, and elsewhere around the world.

Fisher House
fisherhouse.org/
The Fisher House program is a private-public partnership that supports America's military in their time of need. The program recognizes the special sacrifices of our men and women in uniform and the hardships of military service by meeting a humanitarian need beyond that normally provided by the Department of Defense. These homes enable family members to be close to a loved one at the most stressful time—during the hospitalization for an unexpected illness, disease, or injury.


## Give the Gift of Groceries!

www.commissaries.com/certificheck/index.htm
A new partnership between CertifiChecks, America's hometown gift certificate resource center, the United Service Organizations (USO), the Air Force Aid Society (AFAS), Fisher House Founda-

tion, Inc., and the Defense Commissary Agency (DeCA) lets every American make a significant material contribution to the morale and well-being of military personnel at home and across the globe.

## SEND BOOKS

If you are a soldier currently serving in Iraq and would like a free copy of either *Dude, Where's My Country?* or a *Bowling for Columbine* DVD, please send us an email including your full name, your address in Iraq, and all other information we need in order to get it to you.

If you would like to send books to soldiers yourself, check out BooksForSoldiers.com where soldiers will post requests for books they'd like to get their hands on, and all you have to do is pick a soldier to send a book to.

Operation Uplink
operationuplink.org/
You can donate calling cards so military families can stay in touch during their extended separations.

Operation Hero Miles
heromiles.org/
Through Operation Hero Miles you can donate your airline miles to American soldiers so they can get home to visit with their families.

United Services Organization: Care Packages (703-696-2628)
usometrodc.org/care.html#support
You can donate money to the USO to help sponsor care packages
sent to the troops through their site.

Armed Forces Emergency Relief Funds
afrtrust.org/
Each branch of the armed services has an emergency relief fund.
Their money goes to help the soldiers and families with paying
for food and rent, medical and dental expenses, personal needs
when pay is delayed, and funeral expenses.

Red Cross: Helping Military Families
redcross.org
Contact your local Red Cross chapter and find out how you can
help the military families in your area who are struggling in this
time of war.

## CONTACT YOUR ELECTED REPRESENTATIVE

congress.org/congressorg/home/
Let your elected representatives, including members of Congress
and George W. Bush, know what you think about the war.

## SEND A MESSAGE TO OUR TROOPS

anyservicemember.navy.mil/
Operation Dear Abby allows for ordinary citizens to send messages of support and comfort to servicemen and -women stationed all over the world.

# How to Help Iraqis Affected by This War

The American Friends Service Committee
afsc.org
The American Friends Service Committee (the Quakers) funds small, specific projects with groups that are underserved by larger organizations in Iraq. They focus on groups that contribute to building civil society and are a stabilizing influence in their communities.

Oxfam International
Children on the Streets of Baghdad
oxfam.org
Oxfam is helping to provide children on the streets of Baghdad with food, medical care, relief supplies, and the means to be reunited with their families. Read more.

All Our Children
allourchildren.org/
All Our Children is a campaign to provide critical health care to vulnerable children in Iraq.

MercyCorps
mercycorps.org
Mercy Corps works with conflict-affected communities to meet their urgent needs, while providing a foundation for the development of economic opportunities and civil society.

Medical Aid for Iraqi Children
www.maic.org.uk
Medical Aid for Iraqi Children (MAIC) is committed to providing pediatric hospitals with the equipment they need to treat the youngest, most vulnerable victims of this war.

CARE
care.org
CARE focuses on improving the quality of water and sanitation, health care and education for ordinary Iraqis.

Human Relief Foundation
www.hrf.co.uk
Human Relief Foundation, through its Rebuilding Humanity in Iraq program, has been working to provide immediate relief to those suffering the horrors of war while at the same time investing in the infrastructure of Iraq. In this effort, HRF is currently delivering food and medical equipment to thousands in Iraq, as well as continuing to sponsor two hospitals and eight schools in the country.

## WHAT YOU CAN DO TO
## HELP END THE WAR IN IRAQ

1. Vote. In a country where not even 50 percent of eligible voters voted in the last election, the single most important thing that you can do as an American citizen is take part in our democracy.

2. Read and get informed. We're lucky to live in a time where the world's newspapers, magazines, and opinion journals are just a mouse click away: you just need to take advantage.

3. Contact your congressman or congresswoman and your senators expressing your desire for an end to this unjust war. Tell them that the lies of this administration have been exposed and we want our sons and daughters and brothers and sisters back home.

4. Find a peace group in your area and get involved. United for Peace & Justice's website (http://www.unitedforpeace.org/) has a complete guide to finding Peace and Justice groups in your area.

# READ MORE IN PENGUIN

In every corner of the world, on every subject under the sun, Penguin represents quality and variety – the very best in publishing today.

For complete information about books available from Penguin – including Puffins, Penguin Classics and Arkana – and how to order them, write to us at the appropriate address below. Please note that for copyright reasons the selection of books varies from country to country.

**In the United Kingdom**: Please write to *Dept. EP, Penguin Books Ltd, Bath Road, Harmondsworth, West Drayton, Middlesex UB7 0DA*

**In the United States**: Please write to *Consumer Services, Penguin Putnam Inc., 405 Murray Hill Parkway, East Rutherford, New Jersey 07073-2136.* VISA and MasterCard holders call 1-800-631-8571 to order Penguin titles

**In Canada**: Please write to *Penguin Books Canada Ltd, 10 Alcorn Avenue, Suite 300, Toronto, Ontario M4V 3B2*

**In Australia**: Please write to *Penguin Books Australia Ltd, 487 Maroondah Highway, Ringwood, Victoria 3134*

**In New Zealand**: Please write to *Penguin Books (NZ) Ltd, Private Bag 102902, North Shore Mail Centre, Auckland 10*

**In India**: Please write to *Penguin Books India Pvt Ltd, 11 Community Centre, Panchsheel Park, New Delhi 110017*

**In the Netherlands**: Please write to *Penguin Books Netherlands bv, Postbus 3507, NL-1001 AH Amsterdam*

**In Germany**: Please write to *Penguin Books Deutschland GmbH, Metzlerstrasse 26, 60594 Frankfurt am Main*

**In Spain**: Please write to *Penguin Books S. A., Bravo Murillo 19, 1°B, 28015 Madrid*

**In Italy**: Please write to *Penguin Italia s.r.l., Via Vittorio Emanuele 45/a, 20094 Corsico, Milano*

**In France**: Please write to *Penguin France, 12, Rue Prosper Ferradou, 31700 Blagnac*

**In Japan**: Please write to *Penguin Books Japan Ltd, Iidabashi KM-Bldg, 2-23-9 Koraku, Bunkyo-Ku, Tokyo 112-0004*

**In South Africa**: Please write to *Penguin Books South Africa (Pty) Ltd, P.O. Box 751093, Gardenview, 2047 Johannesburg*

# MICHAEL MOORE

**DUDE, WHERE'S MY COUNTRY?**

'Michael Moore is the sand in the underpants of the Bush administration'
*Observer*

'Washington's No.1 pain in the jacksie ... *Dude* is a call to arms, a guide book on how to win the debate with right-wingers and generally a good laugh'
*Daily Mirror*

He's the man *everyone's* talking about. He's taken on gun freaks, stupid white men and corporate crooks. Now Michael Moore is on a new mission: to get us off our behinds and kicking out the corrupt political elites who rule our lives.

*Dude* gives *you* the ammunition: why it's time for regime change at Number Ten; the whoppers spun to wage war on Iraq and make a killing; the 'special relationship' between George of Arabia and the Bin Ladens; obscene tax breaks for the rich – and how Mike's going to get everybody together to get rid of Dubya. Not to mention how to stop terrorism (stop terrorizing Third World countries!), talk to your conservative brother-in-law and get non-voters voting. It's time to stop bitching, get reading – and get your country back.

'Furiously funny' *Evening Standard*

'Shocking, devastating, genuinely funny ... What Moore has to say needs saying again and again. Having read this book, I would even vote for him' *Guardian*

'Rich with facts, gags, self-deprecation and righteous indignation ... it will rouse readers here and in the US to timely revolt' *Independent*

# MICHAEL MOORE

**THE OFFICIAL FAHRENHEIT 9/11 READER**

The Must-Read Book of the Must-See Box Office Smash

'Everyone's talking about Fahrenheit 9/11 … it's the most powerful film I've seen' *Observer*

Bush-blasting, box office-busting, Oscar storming: Mike's turning up the heat …

*Fahrenheit 9/11* is the scorching cinema sensation that has sent waves of shock and awe across the globe. Now *you* can get the facts behind the most talked about film of the year. Here Mike gives you the full, explosive transcript of the smash hit that's got the phoney President running for the hills – with extra outtakes that never made the final cut. He fires back at the critics with his own 'Fact Bible' to prove that it's all true, and gives us just a taste of the buzz that's made this movie torpedo all predictions and become a worldwide phenomenon.

This is *the* book you must read to get the whole story of the film they didn't want you to see …

'Incendiary … gripping … exhilarating … brilliant and brazen' *Guardian*

'You've *got* to see this film' *Evening Standard*

'A blistering Molotov cocktail of a film' *Time Out*

'Tragic, funny, heartbreaking and endlessly entertaining. *Fahrenheit 9/11* is Hollywood's real scary movie' *Heat*